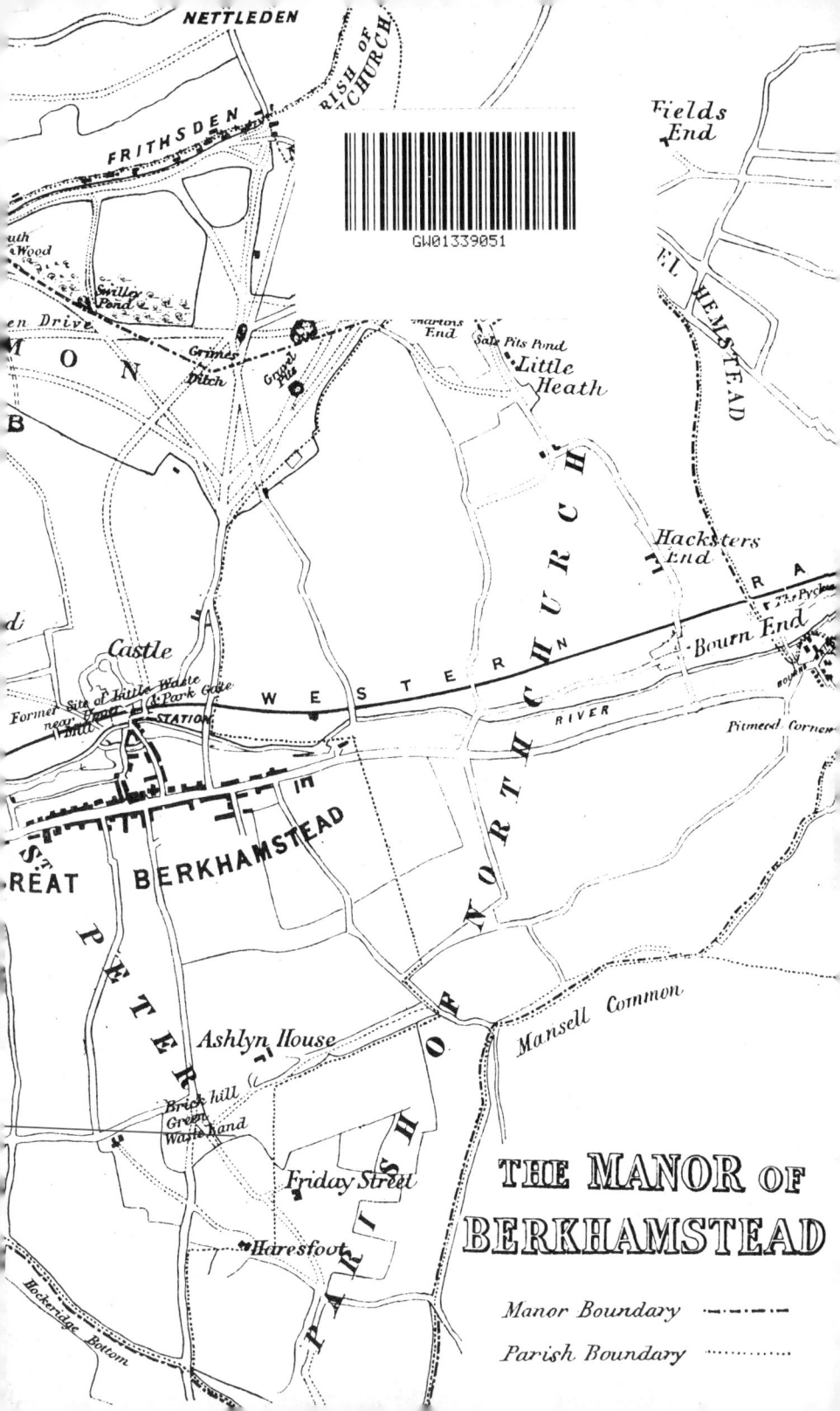

THE MANOR OF BERKHAMSTEAD

Manor Boundary ———
Parish Boundary ·······

A SHORT HISTORY OF BERKHAMSTED

A Short History of Berkhamsted

by
PERCY C. BIRTCHNELL

The
BOOK STACK

© The Bookstack
248 High Street
Berkhamsted, Herts
HP4 1AG

First published 1960

This much enlarged and revised edition
First published 1972
Reprinted 1988

ISBN 1−871372−00−3

Printed by Billing & Sons Ltd, Worcester

Contents

	Author's Note	page 9
I	Through the Centuries	11
II	Berkhamsted Castle	18
III	Churches and Hospitals	29
IV	The Parish Chest	40
V	The Town's Schools	45
VI	From Borough to Urban Council	56
VII	Industries and Crafts	68
VIII	Market, Shops and Inns	75
IX	River, Road, Canal and Railway	82
X	Ashridge	90
XI	The Common and the Park	94
XII	In Stuart Times	100
XIII	The Sayer Almshouses	105
XIV	Literary Links	107
XV	Some Unusual People	111
XVI	Customs and Legends	117
XVII	Local Names	121
XVIII	Manorial and Parochial Boundaries	124
	For Further Reading	125
	Index	126

NOTES ON ILLUSTRATIONS

The original painting of Berkhamsted in the late seventeenth century, by John Wycke the Younger, is at Tresco Abbey, Isles of Scilly, and is reproduced by kind permission of Lt.-Comdr. T. M. Dorrien-Smith.

The portrait of Augustus Smith (in Deans' Hall, Berkhamsted School) was painted by Margaret Woods from a portrait at Tresco Abbey and various photographs.

The portrait of Thomas Bourne (artist not known) is taken from an oil painting which has been in Berkhamsted since 1764; it is now at the Thomas Bourne School.

The excellent drawings of St. Mary's Church, Egerton House, Sayer almshouses, old railway station and Back Lane are by J. C. Buckler; a fine set of his works is at the County Record Office, Hertford.

The artist who included a cow in the picture of Berkhamsted School in early Victorian days was J. Greenwood.

George Dodgson's view of the canal and railway, showing a train at the station, comes from Thomas Roscoe's book, *The London and Birmingham Railway*, published in early Victorian times. The 'Harvey Coombe' locomotive, in the cutting near Gravel Path bridge, is taken from J. C. Bourne's drawing of 1837.

The early view of St. Peter's Church from Castle Street is from Clutterbuck's *History of Hertfordshire*. The view of the High Street (facing p. 32) is from one of Rock & Co.'s letter-headings, which were popular before the days of illustrated postcards. The curious 'Prospect of Berkhamsted,' p. 104, is from Stukeley's *Itinerary*. Mr. C. Howe drew the Market House and Five Bells Inn (p. 76) from an old print; I cannot trace the origin of Peter the Wild Boy's portrait and the drawing of Cowper's birthplace. Mr. E. Williams drew the lace-maker's token, p. 71.

PHOTOGRAPHS

William Claridge (1796-1876), a local artist, probably painted the early picture of the Bourne School. Claridge was also a pioneer photographer of considerable skill: his earliest known prints date from the mid-1850s. Three portraits, facing p. 112, are of his charwoman (not named), an old carpenter (not named) and John Ghost, the parish gravedigger. Other photographs by Claridge are: Bourne scholar, Town Hall, St. Peter's Church before the 1870 restoration, view from Gravel Path bridge, and the earlier of the two Castle Street photographs.

J. T. Newman (1860-1937) was a professional photographer whose prints were published in journals all over the world. His studio was in Incent's House, opposite St. Peter's Church. His portraits, wild life and rural scenes are of outstanding quality and interest. Newman also recorded every important happening in and around Berkhamsted. Specimens of his work are the old police station, King's Road, the later view of Castle Street, the cattle market, Watermill, Billet Lane, 'Gamma' airship, and Inns of Court Regiment.

MAPS

A reduced section of a map by Andrew Dury and John Andrews appears on p. 14; complete sets of three editions of 1766, 1777 and 1782 are in the County Record Office.

See p. 124 for notes on the end-paper map.

List of Illustrations

	Between pages
The earliest view of Berkhamsted	16—17
Aerial view of Berkhamsted Castle	,,
St. Peter's Church, three views	32—33
St. Mary's, Northchurch, 1838	,,
Berkhamsted School in early Victorian times	48—49
Bourne School, Thomas Bourne, and schoolboy	,,
King's Road and the old Police Station	64—65
Castle Street, c. 1860	,,
Castle Street showing 'sunken cottages,' 1900	,,
Market House and Five Bells Inn	76
The 'Harvey Coombe' locomotive, 1837	88—89
View from Gravel Path bridge, c. 1870	,,
Canal and Railway, c. 1840	,,
The original Railway Station	,,
Back Lane, showing One Bell public-house	,,
Augustus Smith	96—97
Town Hall in 1860	,,
Prospect of Berkhamsted, 1724	104
Egerton House, 1832	104—105
'Gamma' airship in Castle grounds, 1913	,,
The Cattle Market, early 1900s	,,
Court Theatre, c. 1920	,,
Inns of Court Regiment, 1916	,,
Sayer Almshouses, 1830	,,
The old Rectory, birthplace of William Cowper	107
Peter the Wild Boy and Victorian 'characters'	112—113
The old water mill in Mill Street	,,
Bulbourne flowing over Billet Lane, 1888	,,

MAPS AND PLANS

Berkhamsted in late Eighteenth Century	14
Berkhamsted Castle, c. 1607	25
St. Peter's Church	30
St. Mary's Church	36
Plan of Manor of Berkhamsted	End-papers

Author's Note

I WAS BORN in Berkhamsted in 1910, started writing articles about the town's history at the age of fifteen, and have yet to break the habit. The rewards for long service are many. Knowing my interest in local history, hundreds of people have brought along old books, diaries, papers and pictures, drawn upon long memories, or dropped hints which started new lines of thought. Sometimes I see myself in the role of a detective, picking up a clue here, a clue there, going on some wild-goose chases but occasionally making a discovery which to me, if to no one else, is rather exciting. And the pleasure is unending; history is being made all the time.

It would have been easier to write a 500 page volume than to condense so much material into this rather slim book, but there is a constant demand for a *Short History of Berkhamsted* at a reasonable price, and I hope that this book will prove as acceptable as a much smaller edition which appeared in 1960 and was out of print by 1966.

The town deserves not one book but several—one on the Castle, another on Berkhamsted School, a revised version of R. A. Norris's *History of St. Peter's Church,* and a reprint of G. H. Whybrow's *History of Berkhamsted Common.* Ashridge, too, merits a long history as well as so many short ones. Perhaps this book will encourage others to specialise in one subject or another.

It may be thought that I should have given more space to weighty subjects and less to trivialities; my reply is that many more requests are received for information about Peter the Wild Boy than about the Black Prince or William Cowper! The occasional repetition of a fact which appears in another chapter may also cause surprise, but this is done deliberately, to save too many cross references.

It is impossible to name even a tenth of the people who have plied me with information, but an especial word of thanks is due to Col. A. L. Wilson for adding greatly to my knowledge of the history of Berkhamsted School. I have also had the privilege of drawing upon manuscripts and notes of the late Mr. Edward Popple and the late Mr. G. H. Whybrow. A number of references in this book to John Cobb and Henry Nash indicate my indebtedness to two excellent Victorian historians.

It is my hope that the hundreds of articles I have contributed to the *Berkhamsted Review* since 1942 will be of value to future local historians.

P.C.B.

I
Through the Centuries

ONE OF THE GREAT EVENTS which made 1066 the best-remembered date in English history took place at Berkhamsted. Here the Saxons ceded victory to the Normans, and from that time onwards bountiful sources of information are available to local historians. In contrast, little is known of life in the district before the Norman Conquest.

The most conspicuous relic of early times, Grims Dyke, may be seen on Berkhamsted Common. A well-preserved section of this boundary ditch, probably Saxon, runs from Potten End to the Nettleden road. Portions of another and much older ditch survive on the opposite side of the valley.

Fork, plough and bulldozer occasionally turn up a coin, implement or some other object that was used long before the Saxons gave Berkhamsted its name. At various times Romano-British remains have been found between the railway station and Billet Lane; in 1933 five Samian bowls were dug up on the gasworks site. Higher up the hill, Belgic ware was found by the local archaeological society within weeks of its formation in 1971; in the same year, men digging a deep ditch through Berkhamsted Park uncovered some Roman bricks.

A short distance from the Roman road which determined the straight line of the present highway, Roman bricks, tiles, potsherds and a coin of AD 270 were discovered when a field behind the Old Grey Mare was ploughed for the first time. During the 1914–18 war, soldiers making practice trenches on Berkhamsted Common found Roman pottery. A more rewarding discovery followed in 1927; part of the substructure of a large Roman building, with dressed flint walls, tesselated pavements and a hypocaust heating system, was uncovered when the golf club made a new green on the Common, near Frithsden Beeches. The site has yet to be properly investigated.

At least we know where a few people lived in Roman times. Not a trace has been found of the homes of the Saxons, who used timber almost exclusively for domestic buildings. Because St. Mary's Church is said to contain Saxon walls, it has been suggested that the largest settlement was at Northchurch. But if, as many people believe, the fortified hall of the Saxon lord of the manor stood on the site of the Norman castle, it is likely that many people lived near the hall.

Like all pioneers, the Saxons cut down trees and burnt scrub, clearing hundreds of acres before the Norman Conquest. Oats, rye, barley and wheat were grown on the ploughland, oxen and other animals grazed in the water meadows, and a large number of swine rooted for mast in the uncleared forest land, from which timber, fuel and game were taken. By the mid-eleventh century, several hundred people lived in the manor. Privileges enjoyed during the reign of Edward the Confessor are mentioned but not specified in Henry II's charter of 1156.

Wherever the lord of the manor's hall was situated, it is reasonable to assume that it was the place where the course of English history was changed in 1066. Having won the Battle of Hastings, the Normans crossed the Thames at Wallingford and then turned eastward over the Chilterns, causing devastation wherever they went. A few days before Christmas, the Saxons rode out from London to parley with William, meeting him at Berkhamsted. Archbishop Aldred, the Atheling Edgar (heir of the Saxon royal line), Earl Edwin, Earl Morcar and the chief men of London swore loyalty to William and in return received a promise of good government. Thus William of Normandy became William the Conqueror at Berkhamsted. A few days later, he was crowned at Westminster.

William granted Berkhamsted, with many other manors, to his half-brother, Robert, count of Mortain. Massive earthworks were thrown up for what was to become a great castle, though the first buildings were of wood. A ditcher, presumably the man in charge of the earthworks, is mentioned in Domesday Book (1086); another entry tells us that there was a large vineyard at Berkhamsted, one of a total of 38 recorded in the whole country. A translation of the Berkhamsted entry is as follows:

XV. THE LAND OF THE COUNT OF MORTAIN.

In Tring hundred. The Count of Mortain holds Berkhamsted. It is assessed at 13 hides. There is land for 26 plough-teams. In demesne 6 hides, and there are 3 plough-teams, and there could be 3 others. There, a priest with 14 villeins and 15 bordars have 12 plough-teams, and there could be another 8. There, 6 serfs, and a certain ditcher has half a hide, and Rannulf, a serving-man of the count, 1 virgate. In the 'burbium' of this vill 52 burgesses who render £4 from toll, and they have half a hide, and 2 mills yielding 20s. There, 2 arpents of vineyard. Meadow for 8 plough-teams. Pasture for the livestock of the vill. Wood for 1,000 swine and 5s. In all it is worth £16. When he received it, £20. In the time of King Edward, £24. Edmar, a thegn of Earl Harold, held this manor.

An enthusiastic local historian may exaggerate the importance of Berkhamsted Castle in national history, but no one can deny that much of the town's early history and many of the town's famous names would be lacking if the castle had never existed. It brought extra trade to Berkhamsted, making it a good market town at a very early date. But for the castle's links with royalty, it is doubtful whether Berkhamsted would have received its early charters. It is possible that the building of a parish church of exceptionally large size was due in some measure to rich occupants of the castle, in particular Geoffrey Fitz Piers, Earl of Essex, who also founded two hospitals and the Brotherhood of St. John Baptist. Many years later the lands of the Brotherhood helped to endow Berkhamsted School, the founder of which was the son of the secretary to the last occupant of the castle. Another rich man who lived at the castle, Edmund, Earl of Cornwall, founded Ashridge. Thus two great surviving institutions, Berkhamsted School and Ashridge, may be linked with the castle.

No doubt many of the men who built the stone walls of the castle also helped to build the two churches of St. Peter and St. Mary. Whether Castle Street was made before or after St. Peter's was built is not known, but as the ancient road from Windsor, which now terminates at the bottom of Chesham Road, is exactly in line with the original entrance to the castle, it is likely that in early times the road continued straight on to the castle. If that was so, the church was built at the crossroads, and Castle Street as we know it today probably originated after the church was built.

The closing of the castle in 1495 must have been a blow to the pride and prosperity of royal Berkhamsted. The market declined and there is a wistful note in a manorial survey of 1616 about the town's 'great Trading and flourishing Estate at such Time as the Castle was maintained and inhabited or much frequented by the Kings of this Realm.'

In the sixteenth century, while builders helped themselves to the masonry of the abandoned castle, Berkhamsted acquired a grammar school, a market house, a court house, and a great Elizabethan mansion, Berkhamsted Place. Less is heard about great personages and more about the ordinary people and everyday affairs of the town. The vestry became an important unit of local government. Parliament demanded the appointment of stonewardens to look after the highways, and overseers of the poor to collect and disburse the poor rate.

In 1618, James I gave Berkhamsted a charter of incorporation, but the extra privileges that were granted were of little practical value. In a less troubled century, no doubt Berkhamsted would have maintained its high civic status, but the bailiff and burgesses lost heart during the Civil War and Commonwealth. There is a familiar ring about their complaints of inadequate sources of revenue and requests for extended boundaries. The Corporation ceased to exist a few years after Charles II was restored to the throne.

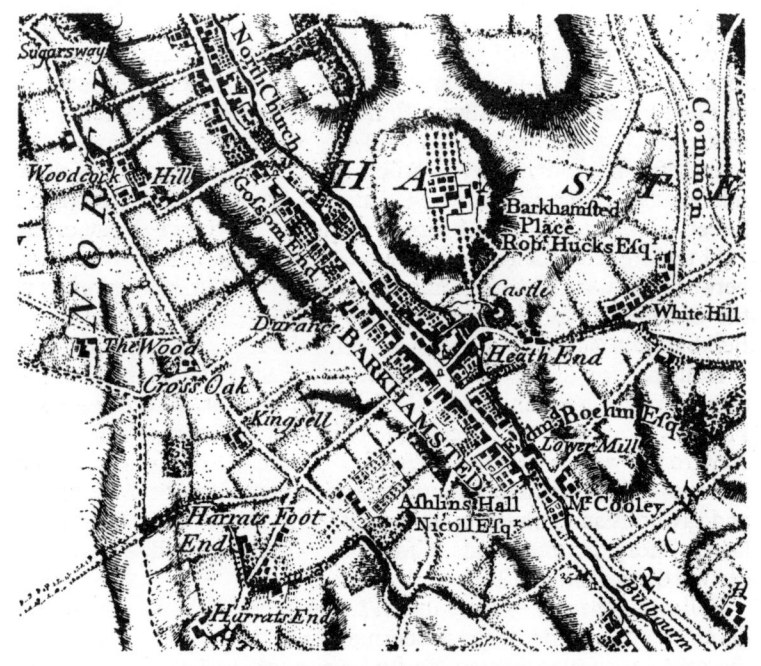

Berkhamsted in the late eighteenth century

In the eighteenth century, Thomas Bourne gave the town a charity school, William Cowper found inspiration in the fields and woods near his father's rectory, and rich people built the Red House, Ashlyns Hall, Haresfoot, and other large mansions. It was the age of elegance. The town's 'genteel inhabitants and splendid assemblies' impressed one writer of the period. A less refined but jollier description appears in the Diary of John Yeoman, a Somerset man, who spent a short holiday here in 1774 and found the people 'as countryfied as in any Town I know; they will Stare at you as iff they had never seen no one before.' At a tavern near the market place he enjoyed the company of 'half a score of Men who I believe delight Much in Drinking, Smoking in Particular; they are a Merry Sort of People I do veryly believe.'

For many of the townspeople it was not the age of elegance, neither was there much merriment. Vestry books tell a story of grinding poverty. Whole families were herded into a wretched, straw-thatched workhouse at Park View Road corner, and in despair honest men stole corn and turnips to save their families from starvation. If caught, they were sent to the Berkhamsted gaol,

A SHORT HISTORY OF BERKHAMSTED

notorious for its insanitary cells. There was no well organised police force, and here, as in many other towns, an 'association for the security of the person and property of the subscribers' was formed in 1794, the main object being to find the wrongdoer and prosecute him.

In 1801, Berkhamsted was still a small town, most of the 1,690 inhabitants of the parish of St. Peter (4,363 acres) living in High Street, Castle Street, Mill Street, Water Lane and Frithsden. By 1851 the population had risen to 3,395, the largest increase occurring between 1831–41, a period notable for the building of the railway, the opening of two large elementary schools, and the revival of Berkhamsted School.

Housing conditions deteriorated, however; there was appalling overcrowding, and building on a large scale did not start until the Pilkington Manor estate, east of Castle Street, was sold in 1852. New roads were created in the valley between the High Street and the canal. This became an industrial quarter, with chemical works and sawmills surrounded by streets of terraced cottages. Some years later, George Street and Ellesmere Road extended the town's eastward growth.

Following the sale of agricultural land at Kitsbury in 1868, housing development started in the western part of the town. By the end of the century the lower slopes of a once-pastoral hillside had been criss-crossed by new roads. In this residential district, many large villas were built for newcomers who were attracted by the town's schools and a fast train service to London. The season ticket era had arrived. To provide direct access to the 'new' railway station of 1875, Lower King's Road was built (by public subscription!) in 1885. Previously Castle Street was the only good road to the station; it was lined with shops and at one period had seven public-houses.

Whichever road was taken to the station, one was assailed by the stench of an open sewer known as the Black Ditch. Waterborne sewerage was not provided until the latter part of the century, despite the fact that piped water was available in 1864, fifteen years after gas was introduced.

Social activities multiplied in the Victorian era. Rooms built by the churches and chapels for Sunday schools became little social centres; at last women were able to spend an afternoon or evening in the company of other women, or in mixed company. Men had their pubs and clubs—more than exist today—and the Mechanics' Institute, besides providing reading and recreation rooms for its members, organised lectures, spelling bees, concerts, evening classes, and 'exhibitions of art and industry' which occupied the whole

Town Hall building. Political meetings were always crowded, and many a speaker or heckler was threatened with a ducking in the horse-trough outside the hall, where a drinking fountain was also provided to encourage temperance. Cricket, football, tennis and athletic clubs had very strong followings.

By the end of the nineteenth century the population of the parish of St. Peter was three times as large as it was in 1801. With the formation of an urban district in 1898, census returns must be related to new boundaries. Originally the urban district was limited to 1,035 acres, only a quarter of the size of the parish; the addition of Sunnyside in 1909 and a large part of the village of Northchurch in 1935 increased the district to 1,982 acres.

In the first decade of the twentieth century builders were again very active in the western part of the town. An unusual addition to the town's buildings was a large corrugated iron shed in Cowper Road, grandly called The Gem. It was Berkhamsted's first cinema, and its life was cut short by the opening of a more palatial rival in Prince Edward Street. The Picture Playhouse, as it was called, ceased to be a cinema when the Court Theatre, at the top of Water Lane, opened in 1917. Named after the Inns of Court Regiment, it was occasionally used as a theatre, but was a cinema for most of its forty years. The site is now occupied by a supermarket, while the old Picture Playhouse survives as the King's Hall.

In September 1914, four of the first Kitchener battalions arrived in Berkhamsted. Between 3,000 and 4,000 men were billeted in private houses; they exercised in Butts Meadow and the Park, part of which is still called Kitchener's Field. A month later their place was taken by the Inns of Court Officers' Training Corps; what was to have been a stay of six weeks lasted until the summer of 1919. In this period over 12,000 men were welcomed and admired by the whole town. The respect was mutual. The official history of the Corps credits Berkhamsted with having given the men the time of their lives. But many of those lives were cut short; a memorial on Berkhamsted Common reminds the old and informs the young that 2,000 men who trained at Berkhamsted did not return from the battlefields. Many Berkhamsted men, too, did not come home again; the memorial outside St. Peter's Church helps to explain why the town's population was smaller in 1921 than it was in 1911.

In 1921, the number of houses in the urban district was 1,670, only 23 more than in 1911. Many old properties were in a deplorable state; as many as eight householders shared one water tap. Slowly, then rapidly, new houses were built by the Urban Council and by private enterprise, the Council developing estates at Gossoms End,

The earliest known view of Berkhamsted is by Wycke the Younger, a Dutch artist of the late seventeenth century (p. 18)

(Reproduced by kind permission of Lt.-Comdr. T. M. Dorrien-Smith)

An aerial view of Berkhamsted Castle (Chapter II). *(Copyright, Aerofilms Ltd.)*

Swing Gate Lane and Highfield. Many council houses were also provided at Northchurch. For the first time houses were built in large numbers on the north side of the railway; this development, by private enterprise, was made possible by the sale of the vast Ashridge estate, which extended to the Bulbourne valley.

In the 1939–45 war, British, American and Dutch soldiers trained in the district. They were outnumbered by civilians from London. So many evacuated children were in the town that schools introduced a shift system.

Many bombs fell in the district; a house in Shootersway was badly damaged, and Sunnyside railway bridge was blown up, causing the derailment of a train, fortunately without serious injury to the crew and passengers.

After the war, building was resumed on an even larger scale, and the population rose from 10,783 in 1951 to 15,439 in 1971. As in the inter-war period, large houses in extensive grounds were knocked down and replaced by homes for dozens, even hundreds, of families. Highfield, Whitehill, Millfield, Cross Oak, Berkhamsted Hall, Northchurch Hall and Berkhamsted Place have vanished. Ashridge is a college, Berkhamsted Hill a research station, Ashlyns Hall a home for elderly people. Kingshill has been acquired by the National Film Archive.

The schedule of buildings of historic and architectural interest is surprisingly short for a town with such a long history. Since the 1939–45 war many old properties, some half-timbered, have been demolished. But all is not lost. The High Street is no longer a quaint hotch-potch of old and new, but its good features are by no means limited to the two ancient parish churches, the row of old inns in the heart of the town, and what is probably the oldest house of all, Incent's, opposite St. Peter's Church.

Often called 'residential' because so many of the inhabitants work elsewhere, Berkhamsted is really a town of great variety. It has good schools, a number of light industries, and the head offices of large business concerns. If no longer a country town in the old, popular sense, it is still a town in the country, blessed with a network of lanes and footpaths leading to meadows and parks, commons and woods. Berkhamsted, in short, is a town which merits the great interest that is taken in its current affairs, its plans for the future, and its long history.

II
Berkhamsted Castle

NOW A RUIN in a setting of great beauty, Berkhamsted Castle is parted by a railway embankment from the oldest part of the town.

No picture of the castle in its heyday is available, but a general view of Berkhamsted by a seventeenth century Dutch artist, John Wycke the Younger, shows an abandoned castle which still possessed massive remains of the keep, chapel and barbican. Despite the lack of detail, one can see how the castle dominated the valley town.

Nevertheless, it is not easy to picture the scene long before the canal and railway were made. The present causeway does not follow the line of the original entrance to the castle. Kings, queens and their numerous attendants rode down Castle Street and crossed the Bulbourne by a low, wooden bridge. Beyond the river the road did not rise as it does today but continued straight ahead over low, marshy ground to a stone barbican and porter's lodge which was not completely destroyed until the railway was built.

From the barbican a drawbridge was lowered over the outer moat, now the road behind the railway. Beside this road a modern flint wall supports one side of the middle bank, on which stood another stone gateway, still a sizeable ruin in late Victorian times. From the middle gateway a drawbridge spanned the inner ditch, giving access to the grand gateway through which the bailey was entered. The bailey was divided between an outer and a much smaller inner ward; from the latter the derne (back) gate led to the park. Within the bailey, surrounded by the curtain wall, were apartments, chapels, workshops, barns and stables. Dominating all the earthworks, all the buildings, a tall stone tower stood on top of the high mound that is still called Tower Hill.

Many writers have suggested that a Saxon stronghold existed on the site, but nothing of pre-Norman date has been found.

Mighty earthworks proclaim the castle's strength as a fortress, but it is better to think of it as a residence, the greatest for many miles around, in the heart of good hunting country. The castle was also an administrative centre not for the town alone but for the vast honour (collection of manors) of Berkhamsted, some of the manors being as far away as Northamptonshire.

Work on the castle was started in early Norman times by William the Conqueror's half-brother, Robert, count of Mortain. Great earthworks were dug and scarped, and a stockade enclosed the hall and various other buildings of wood. Whatever the workmen thought during long periods of forced labour, the final result must

A SHORT HISTORY OF BERKHAMSTED

have left no doubt in their minds as to the might of the lord and master.

So the original castle was not an imposing edifice of stone; that was to come later. But while little remains of the stonework, the Norman earthworks survive except for outer sections which were destroyed when the railway and roads were made. Of course, there were no tall trees, and before pumping lowered the water table the ditches were flooded to a great depth. But even in early times the springs sometimes dried up, and grants were made for cutting grass on the banks.

The banks are steep and difficult to climb; as for Tower Hill, it is doubtful whether visitors would struggle to the top if steps were not provided. Tower Hill is about 45 feet high, with a diameter of 60 feet at the top and 180 feet at the base. The original stone stairs vanished long ago, but massive portions of the steep wing wall survive. The crowning glory of the castle, a three-storeyed stone tower on top of the mound, has gone; even the foundations of the walls are hard to find, but a stone-lined well survives to remind us that people lived in the tower, and that the garrison would not have gone thirsty had they been forced to retire to the last point of retreat. As a reward for the climb there are splendid views, and if the broken walls seem small, the earthworks look impressively large. Not to wander round the moats is to miss the most interesting short walk in the district.

Curiosity is aroused by massive earthen bastions on the north and east sides of the outer earthworks, best seen from the roads which lead to the Common. The suggestion has been made that these bastions were thrown up to create platforms from which missiles were hurled against the castle in the siege of 1216. It is much more likely that they were built to strengthen the outer defences, perhaps serving much the same purpose as towers that were added to curtain walls to deal with attempts to mine or scale the earthworks and walls.

The causeway to the custodian's lodge cannot be dated; it is not shown on a plan of 1607 (p. 25). However, men who plundered the site for building materials probably made a new way across the moats when the wooden bridges were no longer capable of supporting heavy loads.

The bailey is now a lawn, empty but for the lodge and garden and some ruined walls. Broken stretches of the curtain survive, in some places 20 feet high, and parts of the rampart walk may be seen. At the south-east corner the foundations of one of the semi-circular flanking towers have been exposed. To remind us that houses were built against the curtain, the remains of fireplaces may be seen. There are also recesses in the wall which may have been cupboards or garderobes.

The ruins of a rectangular building near the custodian's garden arouse much interest. Recent excavations virtually confirm the belief that it was a chapel. Walls and stone steps extending towards the moat were uncovered in 1972. In very dry seasons, withered grass in the bailey indicates the foundations of walls, but several years may elapse before these signs appear, and it is not known to what use the buildings were put.

Grants of the honour, manor and castle of Berkhamsted were made to one high personage after another, sometimes at frequent intervals. William, son of Robert, count of Mortain, rebelled against the king and lost the estates he had inherited from his father; Berkhamsted Castle was razed to the ground, and the town and manor reverted to the Crown.

Then, in 1104, Henry I gave Berkhamsted to his arrogant chancellor Randulph, who, in the course of restoring the castle, again with timber, tyrannised the workmen. In 1123, knowing that the king intended to visit Berkhamsted after spending Christmas at Dunstable, Randulph stayed in the valley, putting the finishing touches to the castle and leaving a look-out to signal when the royal cavalcade came in sight. When the signal was given, Randulph dashed up the hill to greet the king and had a heart attack; he fell from his horse and a monk rode over him, causing injuries from which he died at the castle a few days later. Berkhamsted was then given to Robert de Dunstanville, a natural son of Henry I.

From 1155–65 the castle was held by Thomas Becket, archbishop of Canterbury and chancellor of England. The oldest surviving stonework is thought to date from this period. The Pipe Rolls show that building on a considerable scale was in progress in 1160. There are references to the king's houses within the motte or mount, and a chamber within the bailey.

It has been said that heavy expenditure on Berkhamsted Castle was one of the causes of Becket's fall from royal favour. He was stripped of all lands other than those belonging to the archbishopric; the king also demanded £300 from him as the revenue from the honour of Eye, Suffolk, and the castle of Berkhamsted, which the king had given to Becket on making him chancellor. Becket replied that he had spent more than that sum on castles and the king's palace in London, but so as not to allow money to be a cause of anger between the king and himself, he paid the sum demanded.

During the tenure of Becket's successor, William of Windsor, £60 was spent on the castle, lodgings, granary and bridges in 1173;

in the following year a new lease was granted to William de Mandeville, Earl of Essex. In the early thirteenth century, another Earl of Essex, Geoffrey Fitz Piers, held Berkhamsted; he founded two hospitals in the town.

About 1189, Berkhamsted was granted in dower to Berengaria, queen of Richard I, but she was dispossessed by King John, whose second wife, Isabella, resided here for a time in 1216, the year of John's death. For some time before and after the end of John's reign, the castle was in the custody of Waleran, a German mercenary soldier.

Orders were given to strengthen the castle, and in December 1216 the defences were put to the test for the first and only time. Prince Louis of France hoped to gain the crown of England by leading the barons to victory against the king; after taking Hertford Castle they marched to Berkhamsted, camping on Whitehill, overlooking the castle.

The garrison, led by Waleran, made spirited sallies, seized chariots and provisions, carried off a banner, threw the camp into confusion and disarmed the barons as they sat at table. However, the barons' mangonels rained great stones upon the castle. On the fifteenth day of the siege the castle was surrendered; the defenders were spared their lives, goods and houses. In the end their cause triumphed, for Louis was driven from the land, the youthful Henry III was on the throne, and Waleran became constable of Berkhamsted and was given a small manor in Cornwall.

For much of the remainder of the thirteenth century the castle was held by two Earls of Cornwall, father and son. Richard of Cornwall, second son of King John and younger brother of Henry III, was a man of great wealth and talent, famous at home and abroad; he was elected King of the Romans at Aix-la-Chapelle in 1257.

When in England, Richard spent much time at Berkhamsted with his first wife, Isabella. They erected a chapel, lavishing much money on its decoration; the hall and the lord's quarters also came in for special expenditure.

In 1243, three years after Isabella's death in childbirth, Richard married Sanchia de Provence, who gave birth to their son Edmund at Berkhamsted in 1249. They built a tower of three storeys in 1254. At Christmas, 1260, Richard stayed with his brother, Henry III, at Windsor, but Sanchia remained at Berkhamsted. She was unwell, and a document states that at Berkhamsted the weather was so fine and mild for days on end that one would have said that summer, not winter, was i-cumen in. Sanchia died here in October 1261.

On marrying for the third time, Richard does not appear to have spent much time at Berkhamsted. But in 1269 the barbican, keep and turret over the sally port were repaired, and mention is made of the chambers of the king and queen, the queen's chapel, and the nurse's chamber. Becket had not been forgotten; a chamber was still known as Sir Thomas's.

Richard of Cornwall paid his last visit to Berkhamsted in 1272. His strength was ebbing, and he died of a stroke at the age of 62. His son and heir, Edmund, also travelled widely; in Saxony he obtained what was supposed to be a drop of Christ's blood and founded Ashridge in its honour.

Edmund died without issue in 1300. His cousin, Edward I, granted the manor, honour and castle in dower to his second queen, Margaret of France. In 1309 she was dispossessed temporarily in favour of Piers Gaveston, whose marriage to the king's niece took place at Berkhamsted. But it was not long before the detested Gaveston, who was created Earl of Cornwall, lost both Berkhamsted and his head. The earldom was once again revived, this time for John of Eltham, Edward III's brother, who held the castle until he died in 1336.

Edward III spent much time at the castle, and during his long reign costly repairs were carried out. One survey states that the great tower was split in two places and needed a new roof. The walls and turrets were in a bad state, the outer gate and barbican were decayed, and much work was needed to restore the great painted chamber and the great chapel. It was an enormous building to keep in repair.

Having been occupied by several Earls of Cornwall, the castle became one of the possessions of the Duchy of Cornwall. In 1337, Edward III made his young son Edward the first Duke of Cornwall and gave him many large estates, including Berkhamsted, 'to hold to him and the heirs of him and the eldest sons of the heirs of the kings of England and the dukes of the said place for ever.'

Six years later Edward became Prince of Wales. Famous in history as the Black Prince, he seems to have been more closely identified with the town and townspeople than any other occupant of the castle. He was very generous to his tenants and especially liberal to the monks of what he called 'our house' of Ashridge. He was also a great sportsman, fond of jousting, falconry, hunting and gaming; perhaps the castle was never livelier than when the young prince was in residence.

When only 16 years old he distinguished himself at Crécy. His archers included several Berkhamsted men and youths: Everard Halsey, John Wood, Stephen of Champneys, Robert Whittingham,

A SHORT HISTORY OF BERKHAMSTED

Edward le Bourne, Richard of Gaddesden, and Henry of Berkhamsted; the last named was appointed porter of the castle, receiving twopence a day and a robe yearly. Several prisoners taken at Crécy were brought to Berkhamsted; ten years later the most famous prisoner of war of all, John, King of France, was taken at Poitiers, treated with elaborate courtesy, and brought to Berkhamsted, where the castle was 'put in readiness' for him. At Poitiers, Henry of Berkhamsted saved the prince's baggage and was promoted from porter to constable of the castle at fourpence a day. Henry died in 1398, and what is believed to be his tomb is in St. Peter's Church.

In 1361 the Black Prince married his cousin Joan, the Fair Maid of Kent; the honeymoon was spent at Berkhamsted, and the whole Royal Family was entertained here for five days.

Created Prince of Aquitaine in 1362, he kept court at Bordeaux, but periodically returned to Berkhamsted. His last visit was paid in 1376; he was then a sick, broken man, and died after a painful journey from Berkhamsted to Westminster.

The castle passed to his son, afterwards Richard II, during whose reign Geoffrey Chaucer was clerk of the royal castles. It is tempting to think that he came to Berkhamsted, but documentary evidence is lacking. It is also pleasant to think of Merrie Berkhamsted, with young men jousting, hunting, and feasting in the painted hall, which was probably so called because it was draped with tapestries; but it seems that there were few occasions for merrymaking during the troubled reigns of the Lancastrian and Yorkist kings. In 1399, on his accession, Henry IV granted the castle to his son, afterwards Henry V, from whom it passed to Margaret of Anjou, queen of Henry VI. Then, some years after the Yorkists' triumph, Edward IV, in 1469, granted the castle to his mother, Cicely, Duchess of York.

'Proud Cis', grand-daughter of John of Gaunt, founder of the House of Lancaster, was the wife of Richard, Duke of York, head of the rival House of York. During the last 26 years of her life, one tragedy followed another. Her son Edward IV and her grandson Edward V died in the same year. Two years later her son Richard III was killed at Bosworth Field. Another son, George, was drowned in a butt of Malmsey. Two grandsons, Edward and Richard, were smothered in their beds. Cicely, however, was spared to see the House of Tudor firmly established; her grand-daughter Elizabeth was Henry VII's queen.

Cicely drew up a detailed time-table showing that she attended one religious service after another. It is a remarkably interesting document; how one wishes that earlier occupants of the castle had left detailed accounts of the way they spent their presumably less religious days at Berkhamsted. Cobb quotes the following Orders and Rules of the Princess Cecill:

She useth to arise at seven of the clocke, and hath readye her chapleyne to saye with her mattins of the daye, and mattins of our lady; and when she is fully readye she hath a lowe masse in her chamber, and after masse she taketh somethinge to recreate nature; and soe goeth to the chappell hearinge the devine service, and two lowe masses; from thence to dynner; duringe the tyme whereof she hath a lecture of holy matter . . .

After dinner she giveth audyence to all such as hath any matter to shewe unto her by the space of one hower; and then sleepeth one quarter of an hower, and after she hath slepte she contynueth in prayer unto the first peale of evensonge; then she drinketh wyne or ale at her pleasure. Forthwith her chapleyne is ready to saye with her both evensonges; and after the last peale she goeth to the chappell, and heareth evensonge by note; from thence to supper, and in the tyme of supper she recyteth the lecture that was had at dynner to those that be in her presence.

After supper she disposeth herself to be famyliare with her gentlewomen, to the secac'on of honest myrthe; and one howre before her goeing to bed, she taketh a cuppe of wyne, and after that goeth to her pryvie closette, and taketh her leave of God for all nighte, making ende of her prayers for that daye; and by eighte of the clocke is in bedde. I truste to our lordes mercy that this noble Princesse thus devideth the howers to his highe pleasure.

Cicely's Rules of the House give details of the times and menus for 'eatynge' and 'fastynge' days, information about the wages that were paid to her servants, and show that some sort of welfare state existed within the castle walls. Sick men were to have 'all such thinges as may be to their ease,' and 'if any man fall impotente, he hath styll the same wages that he had when he might doe his best service, during my ladyes lyfe.'

References to the dean of the chapel, the almoner, the gentlemen ushers, the carvers, cupbearers, cofferer, clerk of the kitchen, marshal and 'all the gentlemen within the house' show that right to the end there was a large household staff.

Cicely died in 1495 and the castle was abandoned. Like many other castles, it was outdated, uncomfortable, and very expensive to maintain. The loss to the economic life of the town must have been considerable; it could not have been easy for the large domestic staff to find fresh employment. But work in the park and in the castle fields continued. In 1503 the underkeeper sent a buck to Windsor for Henry VII's queen, to whom the honour of Berkhamsted was granted. As a child she probably stayed with her grandmother at the castle, but in the words of John Leland it was 'much in ruine' before Katherine of Aragon, Anne Boleyn and Jane Seymour, three of Henry VIII's wives, received grants of the honour.

Builders visited the derelict castle and used it as a quarry. Adding further to the destruction, Sir Edward Cary's masons took away

A SHORT HISTORY OF BERKHAMSTED

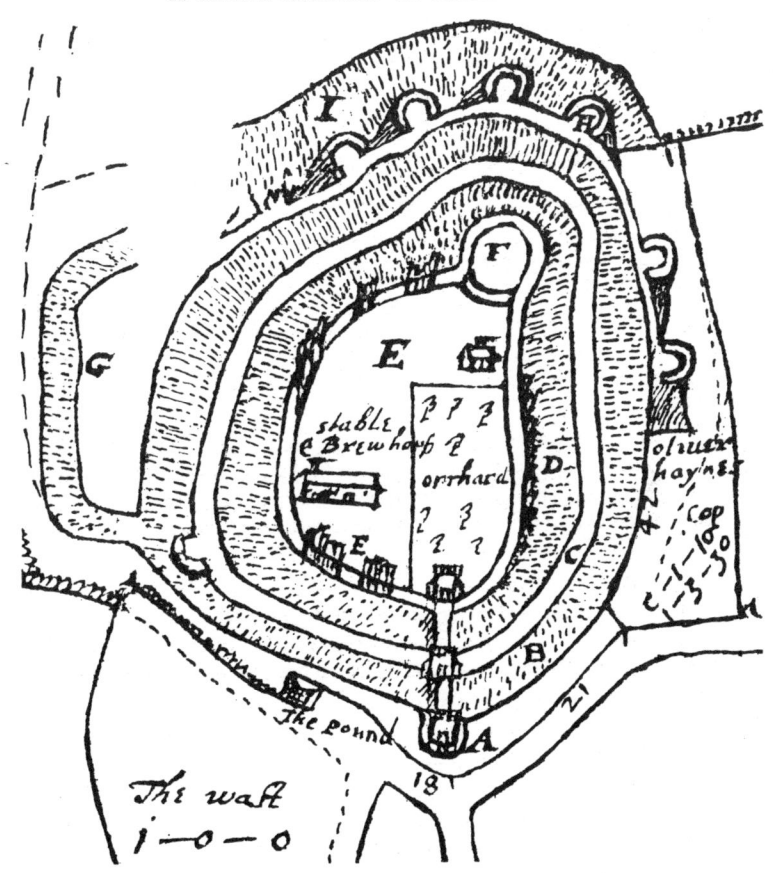

A The porter's lodge and 2 Drawe Bridges with gates & porter's Lodge therein.
B The outer Dytche or mote.
C The Banke Cast out of both the Dytches being a strong Defence.
D The inner Dytche or mote.
E The Castle and E some part of the Castle walls standing.
F a hyghe mounte whereon hath stoode a Tower wch was there last Refuge.
G a Ravelling or Ileand to defend that parte of the Castle.
H The foundations whereon hath stoode strong Bullwark.
I The Counterscarp or outer Dytche, wch Counterscarp and Dytch they would Drowne at pleasure.

The above, taken from a map of *c*. 1607, is reproduced by kind permission of the Public Record Office (Ref. MR 603). Two complete moats are shown and an additional ditch on the west side; this was isolated when Brownlow Road was made and was a watercress bed for many years. It was filled in and built upon in 1961. Mill Street and Castle Street are shown, as well as a track to Berkhamsted Place and the Common. 'The wast' or waste is now called the Moor. The pound, for stray or distrained animals, is now covered by the railway embankment.

much material to build Berkhamsted Place (p. 27). A survey of 1607 says that Cary built 'certain howses for his necessary use within the precincte of the said castle,' and the plan reproduced on p. 25 shows a brewhouse, a stable and an orchard.

Salmon, in 1728, described the castle as 'a building with most of the outer walls and chimneys remaining, and all the windows opening to the inside.' Stukeley said the chapel seemed to have stood near the west wall, where there were signs of a staircase.

A guide book of 1811 mentions the orchard and 'a small cottage with a few outbuildings' on the site 'once occupied by princes and sovereigns.' A rare photograph of 1856 shows sheep grazing on the banks of the inner moat. It seems that the orchard had been cleared by that time; the bailey was already being used for fetes, cricket matches and archery meetings.

Until modern times the ruins and earthworks aroused little more than idle curiosity. Visitors wandered around, picking their way through the undergrowth, dodging heaps of stones and musing upon departed glories. Archaeologists inspected the site and wrote learned reports, but they could do nothing to stop the rot. Great trees crashed down on walls that were infested with ivy.

In the early years of this century, W. Page and D. Montgomerie examined the site and made some excavations. On the motte they found the well, the remains of stairs to the upper storeys of the tower and a fifteenth century fireplace backed by tiles placed herring-bone fashion. Except for the well, all these features have gone, largely as the result of damage caused by trees uprooted in a great gale. Deterioration continued all over the site, and a particularly sad loss was the crumbling away of two large pieces of wall on top of the rampart bordered by the flint wall of the road which runs parallel with the railway. In late Victorian times these two portions, about 8 feet high and 5 to 6 feet thick, were conspicuous reminders of the ancient entrance from Castle Street.

In 1929-31, at a time of much unemployment, a large number of men tidied up the site and preserved what remained of the walls. On behalf of the Duchy of Cornwall, the site was taken over by H.M. Office of Works (now the Department of the Environment). Many large trees were cut down, the walls were protected from further decay, and the moats, once full of coarse watercress, were rendered hygienic. Steep banks on the east side of the arena were removed, exposing fireplaces and a recess in the curtain wall; under a hearthstone, a domino was found in mortar, a homely reminder of a fireside game of long ago.

A yew bowstave, now in the British Museum, was found in the

east moat at a depth of 2½ feet. It is 4 feet long with tapering sides, looking rather like the stave of a barrel. Although the wood on the outer curve is cracked and decayed, the inner face is perfect and the bevels are almost complete. Perhaps it was used in the siege of 1216. In the work of cleaning out the moats, portions of the drawbridge, including a beam 20 feet long, were found. The discovery of some seventeenth century German ware in the sludge suggests that the castle was used as a dumping ground as well as a source of building material. A strange find was a sealed jar of the seventeenth century, full of gooseberries.

The well on the motte was cleaned out and pieces of marble were found in it, as well as lead which may have come from the roof of the vanished tower.

The castle is now immaculate, a haven of peace that is admired as much for its beauty as for its historic interest. Every year many thousands of tickets are issued, apart from admissions to special functions such as fetes and concerts. At rare intervals the castle is the scene of historical pageants. One was held in 1922 to mark the sept-centenary of St. Peter's Church; it was repeated in 1931. An entirely new pageant, in which recordings and floodlighting were used to great advantage, was held in 1966 to commemorate the 900th anniversary of the best-remembered date in local and national history.

An unusual event was the landing in the castle grounds in 1913 of the Army dirigible 'Gamma', captained by J. N. Fletcher, an old boy of Berkhamsted School. Another great occasion was the visit in 1935 of the Prince of Wales, the late Duke of Windsor; he was the first Duke of Cornwall to pay an official visit to the manor of Berkhamsted since 1616.

During the 1939–45 war the castle was again the home of royalty. Great statues from the streets of London were evacuated to Berkhamsted. After the war they were returned, unharmed, to London.

Berkhamsted Place

From the castle many cartloads of worked stones and flints were taken to a hilltop site about a quarter of a mile away and used in the building of 'a noble and exceeding pleasant seat,' known at various times as the Castle, New House, and Berkhamsted Place.

Elizabeth I leased the ruined castle to her Master of the Jewel House, Sir Edward Cary, at the nominal rent of one red rose payable yearly on the feast of St. John the Baptist. About the year 1580 he built the 'fayre mansion' but lived in it for a very short time. Having bought the manor of Aldenham in 1588, he made his home in that village and leased Berkhamsted Place to his brother, Sir Adolphus Cary, who, on his death in 1609, was succeeded by his son Henry, Lord Falkland.

In 1610–11 the castle, manor and lordship were granted to James I's eldest son, Henry, who paid £4,000 for the mansion. Henry died in 1612 and four years later his younger brother Charles (afterwards Charles I) leased the mansion and park to his former tutor, Thomas Murray. Two years after the Murrays moved in, they were visited by Prince Charles (p. 100).

Several changes of occupancy occurred during the Commonwealth. At the Restoration, Berkhamsted Place was the home of the Earl of Portland, but after a fire which destroyed two wings of the house he sold the remainder of the lease to John Sayer (p. 105), who rebuilt the wings on a smaller scale. The only family to stay at the mansion for generations, the Ropers, made little impact on local affairs. In early Victorian times, however, General Finch was a generous supporter of local good causes; he rebuilt the Bourne School and made handsome contributions to the Town Hall building fund. The General and his wife had eight indoor servants; a larger staff was necessary when Berkhamsted Place became the home of Lady Sarah Spencer and Gertrude, Countess of Pembroke. They entertained on a lavish scale, and among their guests were the Duke of York (afterwards George V) and W. E. Gladstone, the prime minister.

In 1946, 'the very choice and compact residential property,' with nine bedrooms on the first floor and five staff bedrooms on the upper floor, was sold. Times had changed. It was not easy to find even one servant. The mansion was converted into flats, and some years later it was left empty and so became a target for stone-throwers.

Faced with flints and Totternhoe stone in chequers 7 inches square, the Elizabethan mansion was probably very attractive before the fire in Charles II's reign. A gatehouse or porter's lodge in the same style survived until the early nineteenth century. In modern times the mansion was scarcely beautified by a worn crust of cement; it seemed to frown upon the castle from which some of its masonry had been taken. Many worked stones, some almost certainly from the chapel of the castle, were found when Berkhamsted Place was pulled down in 1967.

III
Churches and Hospitals

No one knows when the first church was built in this district. Several churches, probably of timber, may have existed before flints were used for the only pre-Norman building of which we have knowledge, St. Mary's, Northchurch. As Nikolaus Pevsner says in the Hertfordshire volume of his *Buildings of England* series, 'the archaeologically, if not visually, most important fact about Northchurch is that the south and part of the west wall are Saxon.'

A priest is mentioned in Domesday Book (1086), and it is thought that his church was St. Mary's. It is inconceivable, however, that people living near the castle had to wait until 1222 for a church that was within easy walking distance.

The *Victoria History of Hertfordshire* makes the interesting suggestion that before St. Peter's was built, the townspeople worshipped in a chapel dedicated to St. James, on the site now occupied by the post office. This chapel had its own burial ground, and at various times human remains have been found on the site. An interesting point is that many parishes held their annual fair on the day of the local patron saint, and as the Berkhamsted fair was for many centuries held on St. James's Day we may link it with the long-forgotten chapel.

The parish boundaries are unusual. The original large parish seems to have corresponded in size and shape to the manor of Berkhamsted. Then, either before or at the time of the building of St. Peter's, a new parish (Berkhamsted St. Peter) was created by taking over 4,000 acres out of the middle of the original parish, which was halved in size and left with a considerable detached portion on the east side of Berkhamsted. This detached portion is now shared by the parishes of Bourne End and Sunnyside.

For hundreds of years the parishes were in the huge diocese of Lincoln; as late as 1842 a cemetery in the town was consecrated by the Bishop of Lincoln. In 1843 the parishes were transferred to the see of Rochester, and in 1877 to the see of St. Albans.

St. Peter's

The large parish church of Berkhamsted is situated in a part of the town which has not changed for many years. It has good neighbours in the Court House, the Tudor schoolhouse, and pleasant old houses in High Street and Castle Street. Part of the churchyard was sacrificed when the highway was widened, and we can only guess how impressive the west front looked before tall shops were built on the roadside green where ancient markets and fairs were held.

No one knows when the first services were held. For convenience 1222 is suggested as the date of consecration; in that year the first known rector, Robert de Tuardo, was instituted by Hugh Wells, Bishop of Lincoln.

In years gone by it was popularly thought that an older church occupied the site, its foundations accounting for the irregular setting out of the present church. People were also eager to give a very early date to a low, blocked arch with roofing tiles in the arch, a puzzling external feature of the west wall of the north transept. For all this speculation, nothing of pre-thirteenth century date has been identified.

The earliest work of all is the chancel, now the Lady Chapel, c. 1200. A little later came the lower stage of the tower, the transepts and the nave. Aisles were added to the nave in 1230, when an addition to the north transept, now the vestry, was made. St. Catherine's Chapel was added in 1320, and St. John's Chantry (now the outer south aisle, largely occupied by the choir) in 1350. The clerestory followed in 1450, and with the raising of the tower to its present height in 1545–6 the church had grown to full size: 168 feet from east window to west door, 90 feet across the transepts, 85 feet from the top of the massive tower to the ground.

'This large and goodly church for the publique service of Almighty

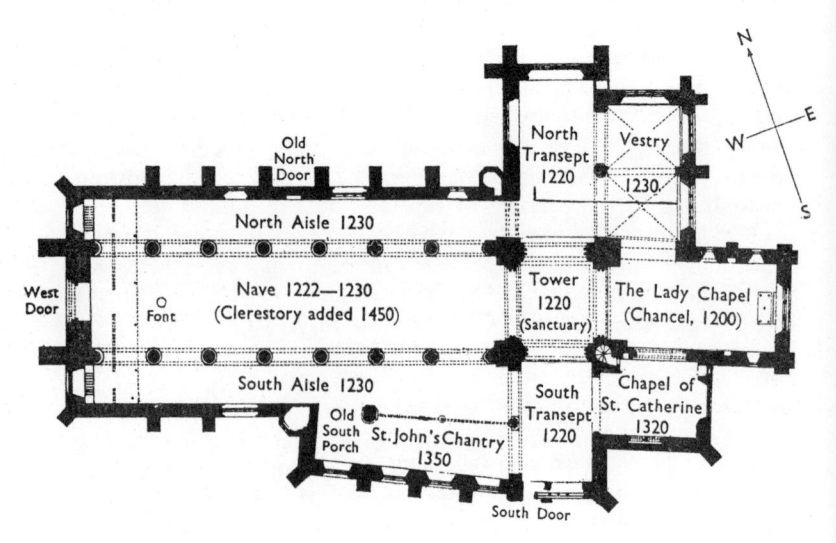

Dates from *Berkhamsted St. Peter,* by R. A. Norris (1923)

God' was found in 1628 to be 'very much and dangerously decayed in many partes.' A century later, Nathaniel Salmon, noting that the chantry of St. John was used only by the master, usher and boys of the grammar school, said that 'as soon as they were all gone into the body of the church, to attend the Catechising, the main beam gave way and the Roof of the Chapel fell in.' On the pillars Salmon saw paintings of the Eleven Apostles and St. George killing the Dragon; these, he said, had 'but lately come to light, having, by the zeal of the last Generation, been whited over.'

Between periods of neglect the church was restored, adorned and occasionally marred. New doorways were opened and old ones closed. Screens and furniture were moved. A musician's gallery was taken down. Monuments were resited and sometimes lost, especially in Wyattville's gratuitous and much-criticised restoration of 1820, when churchwardens and overseers were seen 'tearing down from the walls the memorials of the past.' A few years later, a small house which actually adjoined the church at the south-west corner was pulled down.

Wyattville covered the church with stucco, and photographs show how tawdry it must have looked before a famous Victorian church restorer, William Butterfield, refaced the church with flint. His restorations closed the church for several months in 1870–1, and further improvements were made during the Rev. J. W. Cobb's rectorate (1871–83).

Under Butterfield, both floor and roof of the chancel were raised; the roof of the south transept was raised to its original pitch, the old south porch was made part of the outer south aisle, aisles were extended by knocking down the dividing walls of two chambers at the west end, Wyattville's great west gallery was replaced by the present gallery, the whole church was refloored, and oak benches were substituted for the former pews.

Between 1956 and 1960 external flintwork and masonry were renewed, the tower was given a new timber and lead roof, and the nave roof was completely renewed and covered with copper. The whole nave interior was repaired and redecorated, and the beautiful chapel dedicated to St. Catherine was redecorated and furnished. The most interesting changes were the provision of a new sanctuary in the tower crossing and the resiting of the choir. The cost of all this work was about £24,000.

With new, clear glass in the clerestory, St. Peter's ceased to be a dark church, though for 30 feet at the west end the aisle walls lack windows. Here were the two chambers removed by Butterfield. One, at the south-west corner, was the parish fire station for many years. The words 'Engine House' were painted above a door, walled up in 1871, a few feet to the right of the great west door.

The last vestiges of the paintings on the pillars were obliterated in 1870. In 1960 some medieval splendour was recaptured in the new sanctuary. A reredos screen was adapted from a fifteenth century rood screen, the open portion, backed with oak, forming a series of panelled niches into which finely carved statuettes, formerly at the base of the screen, were placed and decorated in full medieval colour.

Walls, floors and pillars bear memorials to many of the town's worthies, some of whom achieved much more than local fame.

Not every monument bears a name. There is no inscription on the richly arcaded tomb of a fourteenth century knight and his lady. This tomb, opposite the vestry, has caused great argument, and it is now thought that the knight is Henry of Berkhamsted, the Black Prince's constable at the castle. Another servant of the Black Prince, John Raven, is represented by a brass of a knight in armour; it is on a stone pillar in the outer south aisle. It is pleasant to find these memorials to people who were connected with the castle; no doubt kings and queens and princes, though having their own chapel and chaplain at the castle, sometimes worshipped in the parish church with their soldiers, attendants and townspeople.

Above the memorial to John Raven is an inscription in brass to Robert Incent, secretary to Cicely Duchess of York, who bequeathed a cope to 'the parisshe church of Much Barkehampstede.' Robert Incent's wife Katherine is represented in a shroud, with inscription, on the reverse side of the pillar, and it is apt that this couple should be remembered in this part of the church, where masters and boys of the school that was founded by John Incent, son of Robert and Katherine, worshipped for three centuries. The former chantry was separated from the south aisle by a screen which adjoined the fine octagonal fourteenth century oak pillar, one of the most interesting features of the church.

A large marble tomb of John Sayer (p. 105) and a charming monument to John and James Murray, showing the elder boy reading a book, are reminders of some early occupants of the now-vanished Elizabethan mansion, Berkhamsted Place.

In former times many visitors were attracted to the church because William Cowper was baptised there by his father, who was rector of the parish. In the Lady Chapel a tablet recalls the poet's mother, Ann, who was buried in the church with five of her children. The tribute in verse to Ann Cowper was written by her friend Lady Walsingham, and it is read in the light of the large east window which was inserted in 1872 as a memorial to William Cowper.

St. Peter's from Castle Street, 1820

St. Peter's before the 1870 restoration

Distant view before the church was obstructed by tall buildings

St. Mark's, Northbrook, showing village stocks and part of almshouses, 1829.

Unfortunately, it is difficult to see the panel showing the poet at a prayer desk with his hares. In this, the oldest part of the church, a thirteenth century lancet contains fragments of fourteenth century glass, and another bears two royal coats of arms and the arms of Archbishop Chichele (*c.* 1420). On the floor, protected by a carpet, a half-figure in brass of a priest (*c.* 1410) may be that of Thomas Brydde, rector.

Outside the vestry, on the sill of the east window, an ancient brass is mounted on a swivel for the two sides to be examined. On one side is an inscription to a goldsmith, Thomas Humfre (*c.* 1470), with the initial O enclosing St. Jerome. The upper part of the brass has been cut off, and only the lower half remains of a design showing St. Michael weighing souls, and Thomas Humfre and his wife and their nine children, all praying. The reverse side of the brass was used for Thomas Waterhouse and his wife (1559). Thomas was the last rector of Ashridge. Further memorials to the Waterhouse family are in St. Catherine's chapel; the sepulchral recesses and the moulding (original work) above the piscina are interesting.

The large Elizabeth Craddock monument in the south transept bears an inscription which records her gift to the parish; in the outer south aisle there is a kneeling figure to the memory of Mary Isabella Smith (1834), mother of that doughty champion of common rights, Augustus Smith (p. 96).

In the gallery, a decorated board bears the coat of arms of Elizabeth I and the following lines:

> This mighty Queen is dead and lives
> And leaves the world to wonder
> How she a maiden Queen did rule
> Few Kings have gone beyond her.

The arms were cut out of the original large canvas and nailed to the present board, probably at the end of the eighteenth century. The verse, which was almost certainly on the original canvas and was probably the work of a Berkhamsted contemporary of Shakespeare, was copied on wood by a competent letterer. According to early writers, the coats of arms of several monarchs were in the church, and it would be interesting to know where they were stored when Cromwellians were whitewashing the pillar paintings. The royalist relics must have been brought out of some dusty place for the churchwardens to pay fourpence to Thomas Benning 'for sweeping the Kinges Armes in the Church' after the Restoration.

The gallery contains some notable brasses mounted on oak panels. Richard and Margaret Torrington deserve the great interest that is taken in their very early brasses (1356), for their names are no longer linked with the magnificent tomb now ascribed to Henry of Berkhamsted. Another early brass (1360) shows Mary Briggs wearing a plain, graceful dress and kerchief partly covering a reticulated headdress. Richard Westwood is seen in a brass of 1485.

The oldest piece of church plate is a silver communion cup with the date letter of 1569. The peal of eight bells (some recast after the 1939–45 war) dates from 1838, when the tower clock was ordered.

A brass behind the lectern bears the names of many, but by no means all, of the rectors of Berkhamsted. They were presented by the abbot of Grestein, Normandy, until the reign of Edward III; by the reigning monarch until the early eighteenth century; by the Prince of Wales until the local Duchy of Cornwall estates were sold to the owners of Ashridge in 1862; and then by Earl Brownlow.

In early times few rectors stayed for long periods; there were at least 23 in the fourteenth century, one of whom, John of Waltham, was presented to St. Peter's at the end of 1379 and resigned sixteen months later. He was presented to an exceptionally large number of parishes and there is no evidence that he ever came to Berkhamsted, unless he visited his friend, Richard II, at the castle. In 1388 he became Bishop of Salisbury, and received his greatest honour after death, for Richard II ordered Waltham's tomb to be erected in Westminster Abbey. As he was the only person not of royal blood to be buried in the royal chapel, scandalous talk about the king's affection for him continued for a very long time.

At least ten rectors were instituted between 1369–86; Thomas Payne was succeeded by Thomas de Assheford after only nine days. The plagues which persisted after the Black Death probably caused some of these frequent changes.

Thomas Newman, instituted in 1596, was rector for over forty years. His successor, John Napier, would have served for a similar period but for the Civil War and Commonwealth. He was deprived of the living for 18 years, and four men, George Phippon, William Harrison, David Bramley and Richard Lee were 'intruded' by Parliament. But Napier was not treated badly; he obtained a small donative in Buckinghamshire, and although not re-presented to Berkhamsted until after the Restoration, he recorded the baptisms of his eight children between 1648–59, signing the register as rector of the parish.

Another rector whose ministry lasted for over 40 years, Robert Brabant (1681–1722), was also vicar of Hemel Hempstead and chaplain to Queen Anne. Many other rectors held parishes in plurality. Charles de Guiffadière (1798–1810) was also rector of Stoke Newington; for many years he was French reader to Queen Caroline, the wife of George III. As 'Mr. Turbulent,' de Guiffadière figures prominently, and not always flatteringly, in *The Diary of Fanny Burney*.

The favourite rector of local historians is John Wolstenholme Cobb, who wrote *The History and Antiquities of Berkhamsted* when he was curate of the parish from 1853–55 (p.110).

Cobb's predecessor as rector, James Hutchinson (1851–71) provided special services for parishioners living beyond the Common. A curate was sent to Frithsden once a week to hold services in a cottage; services were also held in Potten End school. In 1865, Holy Trinity Church was built at Potten End, and was served from Berkhamsted for many years. In 1895, outlying portions of the parishes of St. Peter and St. Mary helped to form the new parish of Nettleden-cum-Potten End.

A mission room in a coach house preceded the building of a temporary church at Kitsbury in 1890; this is now the church hall of All Saints', a large church which was opened in 1906 and contains a seventeenth century font and a fragment of a Norman font from St. Peter's Church.

St. Mary's

With Saxon features which can be identified only by experts, St. Mary's is the oldest church for many miles around. Though standing more west than north of Berkhamsted, it was known as 'le Northcherche' in 1347, and with a slightly different spelling this became the popular name for church, parish and village, though the old ecclesiastical name, Berkhamsted St. Mary, is still used.

The pre-Norman church is thought to have consisted of a small chancel and an aisleless nave, at the end of which stood a separate chamber about 21 feet square, probably the home of the priest.

The thick Saxon walls of the nave were retained when the present chancel and transepts were added in the early thirteenth century. At the same time a low tower was probably erected on the lines of the old chancel. The present tower was built on strengthened arches in the fifteenth century, and at the same time the transepts were virtually rebuilt.

The cruciform shape was retained until 1881, when what was probably a Saxon wall was removed for the addition of the north aisle. Vestries were also built on the north side of the chancel, and the south porch was added.

On the whole the work of many periods blends harmoniously; few people suspect that the high arcade which was made on the line of the old north wall is Victorian.

Visitors are always attracted by the memorial to a famous oddity, Peter the Wild Boy; his head in medallion is accompanied by a brief biographical note (p. 111). The high quality of the engraving justifies the interest that is taken in the brass. Unfortunately, the worthies of the parish do not have handsome monuments; the tablet to John Edlyn and others, whose family defended common rights, is placed too high for easy inspection. But the doorway of the former rood-loft, high up in the north-east corner of the nave, is too conspicuous to be missed.

The plain font on a modern base is fifteenth century; the same date is claimed for the finely carved Flemish chest in the chancel. Some windows are ancient—the chancel lancet which now opens into the vestry is early thirteenth century—but the glass is modern. Glass inserted in a south transept window depicts a rural scene in which St. Mary's is recognised. This bright, cheerful memorial to Peter Loxley helps to illuminate an ancient stone coffin, said to be a Crusader's, which was found under the nave in 1881.

Another discovery of 1881, a fine seventeenth century painting of the Madonna and Child, found behind the chancel altar, is now in the north aisle, where the altar and furnishings were given in memory of the Rev. R. H. Pope, rector from 1909–31 and previously curate of the parish. A painting of local interest if little artistic merit shows Northchurch as it was in more leisurely days. Also in the north aisle is a tablet to Matthew Brooks, a bellringer for seventy

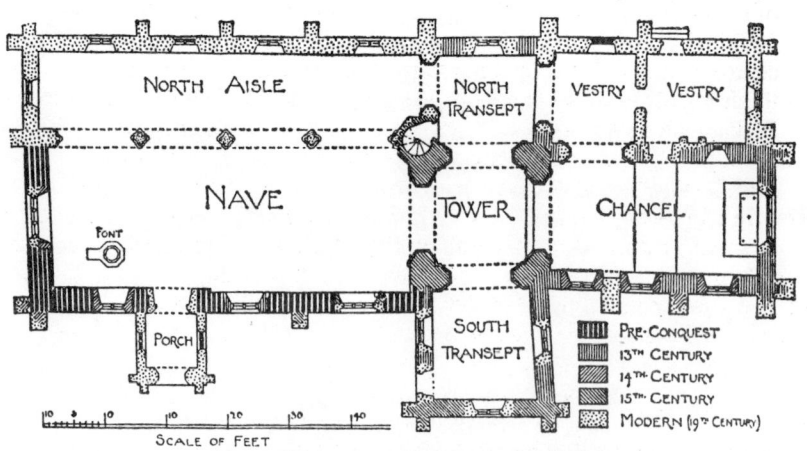

ST. MARY'S, NORTHCHURCH

Reproduced with the permission of the Controller of Her Majesty's Stationery Office from the *Royal Commission Inventory of Historical Monuments in Hertfordshire*.

years. From 1844–1915 he regularly climbed the stairs of the tower, where four of the present peal of eight bells are by Chandler of Drayton Parslow, 1651. The bell frame is inscribed 'TK 1651'.

Ever since the early thirteenth century the advowson has been held by one member or another of the royal family. The list of rectors starts with Hugh of London, 1221, one year before Robert de Tuardo became the first rector of St. Peter's. However, in 1223 Hugh succeeded Robert as rector of Berkhamsted.

The eastern (detached) portion of St. Mary's parish is now shared by the new parishes of Sunnyside and Bourne End. Sir John Hobart Culme-Seymour, rector of Northchurch from 1830–80, built a chapel of ease for his Bourne End parishioners in 1854; this is now St. John's, popularly called Broadway Church. St. Michael and All Angels, Sunnyside, was opened in 1909; it stands beside the older, temporary church (1886) which is now used as a parish hall.

Marlin Chapel

Chauncy (1700) says that several chapels of ease in the parish of Northchurch were demolished or converted into barns. The ruins of one chapel survive in a field near Marlin Chapel Farm; for generations its walls of flint rubble and worked Totternhoe stone, nearly three feet thick, have been crumbling.

The spellings of Marlin (Magdalene) Chapel are legion. Of thirteenth century origin, it seems to have been the domestic chapel of the small manor of Maudeleynes, which was held by Sir Lawrence de Broc at the end of the reign of Henry III. A deed of late thirteenth century date states that Sir Lawrence's son, Sir Hugh, augmented the foundation of his chapel of Magdalene, of which Sir Richard de Berchamsted was chaplain. In 1398, John Clympton, clerk and parson of Maudelyns Chapel, was one of the executors of Henry of Berkhamsted, the Black Prince's constable at the castle.

In the seventeenth century the manor was 'dismembered and sold in small parcels,' and in 1728 Salmon said the old chapel was used as a malthouse.

A moat surrounds Marlin Chapel Farm, which almost certainly occupies the site of Sir Lawrence de Broc's manor house.

Other Churches

The Church of the Sacred Heart in Park Street is the town's most modern church; it was opened in 1967, a large, bright and attractive successor to the Roman Catholic Church in Park View Road which, during the 1939–45 war, numbered among its worshippers General de Gaulle, who lived in a house near the entrance to Ashridge Park. Before the church in Park View Road was opened in 1909, Roman Catholics worshipped in a cottage in Castle Street.

Baptists and Quakers have been active in Berkhamsted for over 300 years. About a fifth of the people of Berkhamsted (and probably a higher proportion of the people of Northchurch) were dissenters in the second half of the seventeenth century. Most of them were Baptists, who met for worship and mutual encouragement in their homes in 1640, if not earlier. The Conventicle Act of 1664 required everybody to conform to the worship of the parish church; refusal could be punished by fines, imprisonment, confiscation of property and ultimately exile or even death. Many local people were prosecuted for not paying rates for the upkeep of the parish church.

Feeling ran so high that a Northchurch man assaulted the rector of Tring to prevent a service being held in the parish church of that town. In 1666, twenty 'malefactors and disturbers of the peace' were found worshipping in a barn at Northchurch; they were given the alternative of heavy fines or three months' imprisonment.

The earliest surviving minute book of the Baptist church opens in this period of persecution. Nevertheless, a membership of 100 was claimed in 1676.

In 1722, Baptists built a meeting house in Water Lane; this was enlarged and used until the present church at Raven's Lane corner was opened in 1864. There are also Baptist churches at Northchurch and Potten End; a small chapel at Frithsden was built in 1834 and closed shortly before the 1939-45 war.

Early records of local Quakers are not available. The present meeting house was built in 1818 and much altered in 1964.

Congregationalists have been active in Berkhamsted since 1790. The first meetings were held in the parlour of a lace merchant named Langston, a close friend of Rowland Hill, of penny post fame. Several other buildings, all in Castle Street, were used until the present church was built in 1867.

Workmen employed on building the railway introduced Wesleyan Methodism to Berkhamsted. Meetings in a private house were held until Prospect Place Chapel was built in Highfield Road; this chapel was used for a few years and survives as two cottages. Wesleyan Methodists built a church in Cowper Road in 1887 and sold it to the Christian Science Society after the union of Methodist churches.

Primitive Methodists held their first meetings in Castle Street, moved to the High Street in 1867, and enlarged their church thirty years later.

The Evangelical Church in King's Road, built in 1874 as 'Hope Hall', was much altered in 1969.

Hospitals

Several hospitals are mentioned in old documents, but the site of only one is known, and its name is perpetuated in St. John's Well Lane, the well having been in the grounds of the hospital.

Founded in the reign of King John, the Hospital of St. John the Evangelist, for lepers, was built on the post office site, part of which was already occupied by the burial ground and chapel of St. James (p. 29). St. James's presumably became the hospital chapel and was renamed St. John's, though as late as 1616 it was described in a manorial survey as St. James's.

Another hospital, for poor and infirm persons, was dedicated to St. John Baptist. Its site, at the south-east end of the town, cannot be traced. Linked with this hospital was the Brotherhood of St. John Baptist, which seems to have been a benevolent society, not a trade guild.

Geoffrey Fitz Piers, Earl of Essex, founded both hospitals and placed them under the supervision of the brethren of the Hospital of St. Thomas of Acon, London. Queen Isabella, widow of King John, confirmed the grant in 1216–17, giving the hospitals the tithes of her mills in Berkhamsted and Hemel Hempstead, three pieces of land, all the dyke work and herbage between the fishpond and hospital, fifteen cartloads of fuel, leaves to feed twenty pigs in the 'hay' and wood, and pannage and pasture for the hospital's cattle in the common pastures of the town. In 1227 Henry III ordered the constable to supply the lepers with four quarters of corn from the grange and two 'bacones.' Six beeches to repair the houses of the hospital were granted by the Black Prince in 1368.

It seems that all the inmates had departed by 1515–16, though services may have been held in one or both of the hospital chapels for a few more years. The Brotherhood still had its own priest in the early sixteenth century, for George Prior, described as the Brotherhood priest, was summoned before the Bishop of Lincoln at Woburn to answer complaints that he was a breaker of the King's peace, a seeker of suspicious and bawdy houses, and a 'pleyer at cardes and alle unlawfull gamys.' He was bound over.

In 1523 the Brotherhood agreed to extend the usefulness of the fraternity by using its income for educational purposes. John Incent was elected president, and for some time a school was held in the Brotherhood house. The sequel is told in Chapter V.

In 1536, a gilt chalice, a mass book, three vestments and various ornaments belonging to the chapel of one of the hospitals were disposed of, and three years later the sale of the lead roof and bells of the chapel suggests that the hospital buildings were then demolished.

IV
The Parish Chest

IN THE VESTRY of St. Peter's Church stands a chest which is believed to date from the early seventeenth century. Soundly made and competently carved, it keeps the contents dry and safe from attacks by church mice.

To local historians it is a treasure chest, and a challenge. It would take months to study all the documents that are kept under triple lock and key.

In the early years of this century a London firm of record agents classified most of the documents under the following headings: 1, Charters and Deeds; 2, Bonds; 3, Rates and Assessments; 4, Apprenticeship Indentures; 5, Removal and Settlement Papers; 6, Bastardy Papers; 7, Letters; 8, Ecclesiastical Papers; 9, Waterworks Papers; 10, Legal Papers; 10, Miscellaneous Papers.

The earliest deed is dated 1296; from 1332 onwards most of the deeds carry seals (some broken) and give family and place-names. Bonds span the years 1600–1715 and, like the rates and assessments, are full of names of interest to genealogists.

Over fifty apprenticeship indentures, dated 1601–1794, show that varied careers were followed by the town's boys and girls. John Stanborowe, for instance, was apprenticed to a 'musitioner' (musician). Many girls served apprenticeships as servants and bone-lace makers, the two duties sometimes being combined.

Letters and petitions deal with a great variety of subjects. A letter concerning a legacy, dated 1596, was written by Robert Wooley to Thomas Waterhouse, a relation of the last rector of Ashridge. A series of letters dated 1618 starts with George Dover's protest against his arrest for debt; the second letter promises speedy payment; the third announces the discharge of the debt. Ecclesiastical papers refer to the release of a number of persons from sentence of excommunication.

The Waterworks papers tell the story of an unusual bequest. Thomas Baldwin, who was related to the Wethereds of Ashlyns, gave to the poor of Berkhamsted, Watford and Rickmansworth 'the benefit and profits of certain springs and waters near Hyde Park . . . which were brought to serve the city of Westminster with water.' This very early water undertaking was sold when George II improved Hyde Park and created the Serpentine lake; Berkhamsted's share of the proceeds (£432) was reinvested, providing annuities to poor persons of the parish.

Baldwin, whose monument in St. Peter's Church is in a much

reduced and mutilated state, also directed that 'as many poor men as I shall be yeares of age at my decease' (20 in Watford, 10 in Rickmansworth and the rest in Berkhamsted) were to have black cloth gowns and 2s. 6d. apiece for a dinner on the day of his funeral. He died in 1642, at the age of 74, so 44 poor Berkhamsted men were entitled to a dinner and gown.

Churchwardens' Accounts

The first book of churchwardens' accounts, for the years 1584–1748, is not kept in the vestry. The 366 folios are in the safe keeping of the British Museum, bearing the inscription 'Purchased at Putticks, December 4, 1851' on the flyleaf. How this valuable book became Lot No. 69 at a public auction sale is a mystery; perhaps it was taken away from Berkhamsted when some enquiries were made regarding the parishioners' rights under the old charters. The book's subsequent adventures are not known.

The first pages are fragmentary and difficult to read, but from 1603 onwards the entries are more easily deciphered. The variety of subjects matches the wide powers of the vestry; information of great parochial importance may be found, but inevitably one dallies over curious items and trivialities, especially those which record wages, prices, and unusual activities.

There are several references to the dog-whipper, a minor functionary who expelled unruly dogs from church, using wooden tongs to grip them by the neck. In the early seventeenth century this task was performed by Thomas Fletcher, who was also required to sweep the market house. He was paid 4s. a year.

In 1601 a new ducking stool was ordered, payments including 1s. 6d. for felling and carting the oak, 8d. for sawing the wood, 3s. to two carpenters who spent 1½ days fitting up the stool, and 2s. 2d. for 'the ground about it.'

In 1603, 'Goodman Scotte,' the sexton, received £1 19s. 4d. for twelve months' devoted service. A carpenter received 7s. 6d. for seven days' work 'to make ye stares that go up to ye pulpitt and ye flower of ye seat appointed for ye minister to sit in.' A bolt for the chancel door cost 1s. 4d., and 10d. was 'payed for an houre glasse,' perhaps to time the sermon.

In 1617, 8d was paid 'for taking down of the maypole and carrying it to the Church.' It was put to further good use, for John Dunn was paid 2s. 2d. for sawing the maypole to 'mend about the church rails and the gutter of the market house.'

While carefree lads and lasses danced round the maypole, destitute old soldiers passed through the town and blessed the churchwardens for gifts from parish funds. In 1622, two poor men 'who had been taken prisoner by the Turks' were given a shilling apiece; a similar gift was made to a man who had been 'in the warres of Bohemia.'

In 1622, 3s. was paid 'for three quarts of wyne at Whitsontide' and 2d. for 'oyle for the bells.' In 1634, when the sexton's wages had risen to £2 8s. 8d., 4s. 8d. was paid 'for bread and wine to make ye children drinks when they went on procession.' For making 'ye little longe ladder' James Baker received 6s. 6d., and men who 'carried stones into ye Church which were blowen off with ye great wind' were paid 3d. In the same year, a shilling was spent on '2 barres to stay the glass in ye schollers chappel.'

Every parish was required by law to provide itself with a net for catching rooks, crows and choughs; an entry dated 1639 shows that 4s. was paid for 'one nett to catch the bird in church.'

Some items of 1660–1:

Item for a journey to Hempstead with hoss, 1s. 6d.
Item pd. for a joint of pork for a Minister that preached on Lords Day, 1s.
Item pd. to Richard Baker for 6 daies and a halfe's work about the Church wall, 9s. 9d.
Item pd. for beer for the workmen, 1s. 10d.
Item pd. in the 2 years to poore travellers that were distressed, £1 3s. 1d.

The bellringers were kept busy in the last two months of 1691. They received 12s. 'at the News of the Limerick Surrender,' 8s. 'at the Return of the King from Holland,' 13s. 5d. for ringing on December 4 and 5 (no reason stated), and 6s. 8d. on coronation day.

The second 'Church Book of Accounts' cost two guineas, was started in 1747, and remains in its rightful place, the vestry.

Payments were made regularly for the extermination of 'vermyn', and many Berkhamsted men and boys (and at least one girl) earned money by producing the heads of hedgehogs, sparrows, weasels, polecats and bullfinches. Some typical payments made in 1735:

To Thomas Peacocks boy for a Hedge Hog, 4d.
Pd. John Binns boy for 12 Sparrows, 3d.
paid Judith Leigh for 2 Poulcats, 8d.
paid Charles Edge for 40 Sparrows, 10d.

In 1767, Charles Cowper, surely not a kinsman of the poet, was paid 4d. for a hedgehog; another entry, 'Paid Old Bird for a Poltcatte, 4d.' suggests that the parish clerk was not always respectful to the aged.

Polecats and sparrows were not the only pests. In 1758 a woman was paid 4d. for 'searching the Charity Girl concerning her not being clean.' Two men who 'watched all Night after John Flaxman's fire' were paid 2s. 6d. For 'summonsing the Parishioners to a Mooting concerning the Rent of the Workhouse,' William Cooper was paid 1s. 6d. in 1753.

Some more extracts:

1758. Expence going to Tring to Treat with a Master abt taking a Charity Boy Apprentice, 1s. 7d.
Gave to sailler by Mr. Johnson's order, 2s.
Gave to a Soldiers Wife by order of Mr. Noyes, 1s. 6d.
Gave to Eggleton Trott when he offered himself a volunteer, 1s. 6d.
1761. Paid for Leather Pipes for the [fire] Engine, £1 1s.
Paid for Beer for the ringers when King George the 3rd was proclaimed 7s. 6d.
Pd. for Musick of ye Kings proclamation, 1s. 6d.
1762. To Henry Grover for Beer on the Coronation Day, 6s. 8d.
1776. Paid for binding Benj. Watriss Apprentice, 7s. 6d.
Paid for a Pair of Shoes for Benj. Watriss, 5s. 3d.

'The Constables' Book of Accompts' (1748-1819) is another interesting source of information. Some extracts:

1748. Mending lock and handcuffs, 1s. 6d.
1750. Expenses when Jane Johns was whipped, 3s.
1785. Expenses taking Rowland and sitting up with him all night at King's Arms, 1s. 8d.
1801. Attending the Magistrates with a woman and giving her money to go out of town, 3s.
1807. Putting a man in the stocks and attending by order, 1s. 6d. New locks for the stocks, 1s. 2d.
1815. Paid John Ludd for whipping a man at the stocks, 3s. 6d.

The Registers

The registers of Berkhamsted St. Peter, started in the reign of Henry VIII, are widely acknowledged to be of special interest and importance. The records are complete from 1538 to the present day, save for the years of the Civil War and Commonwealth and some shorter periods when the parish clerk seems to have been negligent.

The following extracts (most of them tragic) are taken from the register of burials:

1583. A poor woman from hunger [no name].
1598. John Wynche (?), executed for murthering John Bristowe.
1623. Joanne ye wife of Arthur Norkott (murthered).
1629. Robert Wood, who died of the obstruction of his [gullet? gut?] through eating of bread.
1635. Richard ye sonne of Robert Bayly drowned in Brickiln Green Pond. [*Marginal note:* There hath been two drowned in it.]
1635. Susan Wheeler suppose to poyson hirselfe.
1638. William Gooderidge, buryed but yet alyve. [What does this mean?]
1665. Robert Toofield buried, poysoned by his wife, burnt alive at Hertford.
1738. Shadrach, Mesach and Abednego ye sons of William and Anne Plater. [Three boys—triplets?—buried on same day].
1748. Joseph Maritan, a Black. [First and apparently only reference to a coloured man in Berkhamsted St. Peter's.]

The register of births contains some unusual names. Christmas Bird, baptised in December 1769, was not quite so unfortunate as a boy who, on April 22, 1632, was baptised 'What you please the Sonne of William Gill.' Perhaps there was a parental row at the font which ended with father or mother saying, 'Call him what you please.'

Northchurch Records

Northchurch has not been so fortunate as Berkhamsted in keeping its earliest records, but lists of baptisms, marriages and burials are complete from the year 1655. In addition, a few isolated transcripts from earlier registers are preserved, and in the list of burials we find this entry of 1610: 'Mother Clifford born in the time of King Henry the Seventh being an hundred and five years ould and more.'

Several Northchurch parishioners disobeyed the law, designed to protect the woollen trade, that everyone was to be buried in woollen cloth. A rector, the Rev. Francis Ayscough, was probably buried in linen, for his widow 'paid the penalty for not burying in Woollen.' John Puttenham's preference for linen when his wife Judith was buried in 1719 had an unpleasant and costly sequel: William Fenn reported the offence 'as soon as ye Burial was over,' and John Puttenham was called upon to pay £2 10s. 'for ye use of ye poor' and a similar sum to the common informer, William Fenn. John Dicks, a stranger found dying in the snow at the Cow Roast in 1729, was 'neither buryed in Linnen nor Woollen but Straw only and so not contrary to ye Act of Parliament.'

The word 'Poor' was written against the names of 63 of the 108 parishioners whose burials were recorded in 1788–93. In the 1830s the parish clerk noted such occupations as farmer, labourer, plait-dealer, basket-maker, rope-maker, boatman, gipsy, railway inspector, turner, ironfounder and miner, the last-named having been killed while excavating Northchurch railway tunnel. Of the fourteen couples married in 1845, ten bridegrooms were labourers and twelve brides were straw-plaiters.

Formerly Northchurch was notorious for bad drains and epidemics. The registers show that five workhouse inmates died in April 1767, and that between December 1796 and March 1797 five parishioners died of smallpox. The greatest tragedy came in 1832, when, between September 22 and October 10, fifteen Northchurch people died of cholera. Subscriptions were invited to relieve distress, and over half of the £115 raised to help the poor was donated by the Countess of Bridgewater, of Ashridge. Much of the money was spent on blankets, beds, lime, clothing, shoes, tar barrels, and brandy; in fact, brandy was the most expensive item of all, £11 14s. 6d.

V
The Town's Schools

THE SCHOOLHOUSE facing St. Peter's Church is over 400 years old, and for the first three centuries it sufficed for the needs of what is now known as Berkhamsted School. To this day the Tudor building, described by an Elizabethan writer as the fairest schoolhouse in the land, is all that one sees from the top of Castle Street. Lower down the hill the chapel, hall, library and other modern buildings come into view.

The founder of the school, John Incent, was the son of Robert Incent, a wealthy townsman and secretary to Cicely, Duchess of York, at the castle. Robert died in 1485, when John was about five years old, and it is thought that Cicely took much interest in the boy's upbringing.

Contemporary documents show that a house called Incent's stood at the corner of Elvyn Lane (Chesham Road), and the half-timbered house opposite the parish church is popularly thought to have been John's birthplace.

He never lost interest in the town of his birth, and was well aware of the lack of organised schooling in Berkhamsted. He also knew that the Brotherhood of St. John Baptist (p. 39) ceased to serve a useful purpose when its hospital for sick and infirm persons was closed in 1515–16. The office of master had dwindled into a sinecure for a citizen of London who seldom came to Berkhamsted. Fortunately, he was succeeded by John Incent, who, as the new 'pressident and cheafe,' called a meeting of the inhabitants in 1523 at which they agreed to appropriate the lands and tenements of the Brotherhood and devote the rents to a school. Substantially increasing the endowment, Incent gave 'all his lands which he had there by his parents or by purchase.' A schoolmaster was procured and it seems that the scholars were taught in the Brotherhood house.

Fifteen years later, Incent was one of Thomas Cromwell's agents responsible for the sequestration of religious properties and none knew better what might happen to the brotherhood lands. He was appointed to the Deanery of St. Paul's in 1540 and by October the following year obtained a licence from the King to found and build a school for 144 pupils and to endow it with lands to the value of £40 a year. To make assurance doubly sure he went through the motions of buying the Brotherhood lands.

Then, 'not without ye healpe of ye town and country,' he 'builded with all speed a fair schoole large and great all of brick very sumptuously . . . When ye said Schoole was thus finished [1544] ye Deane sent for ye cheafe men of ye towne into ye school where he kneeling gave thanks to Almighty God.' Richard Reeve was then placed in 'ye seate there made for ye schoolmaster.'

The Dean died in 1545, and legal troubles at once began to harass the school's progress. 'Evill persons' claiming an interest in the Dean's estate alleged that the founder had devoted more revenue to the school than was allowed by the Royal licence: but a Royal Commission found that this was not so.

To forestall any future attacks of a similar nature, the master had the school incorporated by Act of Parliament under the name of 'the Free Schole of King Edward the Sixte in Berkehampstedde.' By the terms of this Act, the master and usher (or second master) were made trustees of the school's property; the school received a common seal bearing Incent's arms; the Warden of All Souls', Oxford, became its Visitor, receiving the sum of 13s. 4d. at each visitation; the stipend of the master was fixed at £17 6s. 8d. and the usher's at £8 13s. 4d. Finally 'the residue of the Revenues shall be yerely employed and bestowed in and about the relief and helpe of pore people and the reparations of the House of the said Schole.' The first of these clauses, making the master and usher trustees of the property, was destined to lead to much trouble in the future.

Richard Reeve, the first headmaster, was a noted teacher, but his uncompromising protestantism was such that he offended Queen Mary and was soon replaced after her accession by a more moderate man. The school grew and prospered under the two following headmasters, Saltmarsh (1561–99) and Thomas Hunt (1599–1635), when numbers approached 100 and a number of scholars achieved some distinction.

The history of the next thirty years for the school reflects the troubles in the country at large. There was a procession of masters, none of whom stayed long or achieved anything of note. Beyond their names and roughly their dates, little is known. Inflation had set in and the fixed stipends for master and usher were less valuable than before. It is doubtful if by the time of the Restoration the income from the endowments sufficed to meet the costs.

From 1663–8 the headmaster was Thomas Fossan, who was rector of Little Gaddesden and preferred living there to residence in the school. As his usher lived at Ivinghoe and also seemed reluctant to attend, the scholars were neglected and an appeal was made to the school's official Visitor, the Warden of All Souls. He issued reprimands, whereupon both Fossan and his usher Seare resigned.

A mild revival in the school's fortunes seems to have taken place under Newboult (1668–85) and Wren (1685–91), but during the long headmastership of John Theed (1691–1734) further complaints were

A SHORT HISTORY OF BERKHAMSTED 47

made by the townsfolk to the Visitor, mainly to the effect that the boys were not taught useful subjects such as reading, writing or casting accounts, and also that charges were being levied and that monies from timber sales were being misappropriated.

Visits were paid by successive wardens in 1707, 1719 and again in 1729, but on each occasion the Visitor supported the headmaster against the petitioners.

Theed's successor, the Rev. Evan Price (1735–53) seems to have been a much misunderstood man. A suit against him and his usher was brought by the vestry, who complained that Price had misapplied the charities' funds, that he refused to produce deeds of the estate, that he had failed to appoint an usher until 1743, and that numbers had dwindled to about four. In fact there was no evidence to show that Price had misapplied funds. Under his charter he and the usher were the sole trustees and it was not incumbent upon them to show the deeds to the rector or to anyone else. He proved that he had appointed a kinsman of his own before Allett as usher, and as far as numbers were concerned he blamed the new Bourne charity school.

Nevertheless the suit, once started, dragged on for 100 years, as the Chancery lawyers got their claws into the school's endowments. The poor of Berkhamsted, on whose behalf the well-meaning rector and his fellows had gone to battle, probably suffered most. The case in the long run cost upwards of £5,000.

The succession of headmasters continued, however, and under the Rev. Dr. John Dupré (1789–1805) there was a considerable revival in the fortunes of the school. Numbers were said to be between 100 and 150 round about 1790, and a wide curriculum was taught. It is doubtful, however, whether throughout his mastership Dupré had as many as a dozen local 'foundationer' boys in the school. Most of the pupils came from a distance and were boarded out.

As Dupré charged fees for tuition and boarding, it was not surprising that when he contemplated retiring he should work hard pulling strings to get his son Thomas appointed as his successor. In 1805, Thomas Dupré, at the age of 22, became the eighteenth headmaster. The usher he appointed was his uncle, Michael Dupré, who resided in Hampshire until he died of apoplexy in 1818. Then Thomas appointed a friend who lived in Cheltenham; he remained there, drawing his stipend, until in 1833 he was ordered to go to Berkhamsted to teach. He promptly resigned.

Thomas Dupré had no intention of exerting himself and within a year or two of his succeeding to the headmastership there were no scholars. He refused to teach local boys anything but Latin or Greek.

The townspeople, led by the rector and the churchwardens, made repeated attempts to get the Court of Chancery to force the headmaster to do his duty, but Thomas adroitly countered all their proposals and used the creaking, cumbersome and devious delays of the Chancery Courts to thwart any attempts to end the abuses which he practised in such masterly fashion.

By 1815 he had accepted a living in Lincolnshire and spent much of his time there. He was certainly never worried by such a thing as a conscience. Subsequently he appointed first one and then another son to be usher.

This scandalous situation continued until 1841, when, through the vigorous promptings of Mr. Augustus Smith, the Court of Chancery agreed to a scheme whereby the headmaster and the usher were made to resign. Even then Thomas Dupré received a pension.

To the first two headmasters of the 'new' school, the Rev. E. J. Wilcocks and the Rev. J. R. Crawford, fell the task of shaping its destiny. In 1864 came Dr. Bartrum and for the first time Dean Incent's proposed number of 144 boys was reached and surpassed. During Bartrum's energetic rule began the various extensions which have transformed much of Castle Street and Mill Street.

The school chapel, its design inspired by the Venetian church of Santa Maria dei Miracoli, was the gift of Julia Fry, whose husband, Dr. T. C. Fry, was appointed headmaster in 1887. The number of boys rose to over 400 before he retired in 1910 to begin at the age of 60 a second vigorous career as Dean of Lincoln. He was succeeded by his second master, Mr. C. H. Greene, during whose reign the encirclement of the grass quad was completed by the opening of the Junior School block and Deans' Hall, both begun in Dr. Fry's last year. The Hall, incidentally, is named after both Incent and Fry.

Mr. Greene was succeeded in 1927 by Mr. H. L. O. Flecker, and from 1931 until 1945, a very difficult period, a much-loved Old Berkhamstedian, Mr. C. M. Cox, was headmaster. In 1944, with the introduction of the Butler Education Act, the school, after having been for some years a 'direct grant' school, became independent.

Mr. C. R. Evers succeeded Mr. Cox in 1946 and began the construction of Wingrave. Then, in 1953, one of Mr. B. H. Garnons Williams' first tasks as headmaster was the provision of what was practically a new school, Newcroft, in Mill Street, which was opened by H. M. Queen Elizabeth the Queen Mother in 1958. Many more extensions have been made and continue to be made.

Over 400 years of school history deserve a whole book, not a few pages. It is hoped that the town and school will not have to wait long for a volume which does full justice to the subject.

Berkhamsted School in early Victorian times

The Bourne Charity School and first home of Berkhamsted School for Girls

A Bourne scholar

Thomas Bourne, founder

Berkhamsted School for Girls

In 1887, a revised scheme for the government of Berkhamsted School (for boys) included a clause that 'so soon as the income of the foundation shall be sufficient, the governors shall apply a yearly sum of not less than £250 in promoting the secondary education of girls resident in and around the town of Berkhamsted.' The contribution was in fact £100 (raised the following year to £200), when the school was opened by Countess Brownlow on May 1, 1888.

The school's most persistent champions were Mr. (afterwards Sir) John Evans, the archaeologist, and Mr. Henry Nash, a shopkeeper; it was their task to dispel fears that insufficient money would be forthcoming and to overcome the last lingering prejudices against secondary education for girls. From the start the school has had the same governors as the Boys' School with the addition of four, and in more recent times six, 'duly qualified women.'

The school's first home was 222 High Street, which some years earlier had been vacated by the Bourne School. The classrooms were austere. Miss Charlotte Disney, the first headmistress, presided and conducted her correspondence from a desk on a small platform at one end of an upstairs room where several classes were taught together. One small stove provided inadequate heating and all the girls wore little black shawls. A page-boy in livery carried Miss Disney's books from one class to another.

At the start there were only fourteen pupils, but numbers quickly increased and complaints of cramped conditions were heard. The hall was enlarged and extra classrooms were built, as well as a laboratory which, for reasons of safety, was built in the garden, detached from the main building. The school had the use of tennis courts and also of a swimming bath at the waterworks, where learners were strung together on a rope and pulled through the water. When Miss Disney was succeeded by Miss Beatrice Harris in 1897 there were 80 girls in the school.

A move to Kings Road was made in September 1902, in new premises which still form the central part of the school's present home. Boarders lived on the top floor and the school was carried on below. Miss Harris envisaged 150 girls, but by 1908 she had 200. A new wing was opened in June 1915 by Mrs. Winston (afterwards Baroness) Churchill, who, as Clementine Hozier, lived at 107 High Street and was an old girl of the school. Lady Churchill also attended the opening of additional buildings by Her Majesty the Queen Mother in 1958. Miss Harris was succeeded as headmistress by Miss G. R. Sowels in 1917, Miss C. F. Mackenzie in 1929, Miss B. W. Russell in 1950, and Miss M. R. Bateman in 1971.

Ashlyns School

Young compared with the grammar school in the valley, Ashlyns School occupies modern buildings which were erected for a famous institution, the Foundling Hospital.

For centuries, probably from the time of Reginald Asselyn, who is mentioned in 1314, Ashlyns has been the name of a large hilltop estate. Francis Wethered, Comptroller of the Works to Charles II and an alderman of Berkhamsted, was one of the many owners of Ashlyns. The house in which he lived was replaced towards the end of the eighteenth century by Ashlyns Hall, and for many years it was the home of Augustus Smith. How appropriate that parts of the estate of this great educationist should be devoted to Ashlyns School and to a 'middle' school, opened in 1970, called the Augustus Smith School.

Between the two world wars, at a time of appalling unemployment, Berkhamstedians received the news that the Ashlyns estate had been acquired by the Foundling Hospital. A vast building programme gave employment to hundreds of men, and for several years the history of the charitable institution was continued at Berkhamsted.

The Foundling Hospital was founded in Bloomsbury by Captain Thomas Coram, master of a trading vessel, and the first unwanted children were received in 1740. On admission days as many as 100 women with children were at the door, though there were vacancies for only 20. For a time, Parliament granted the governors £10,000 a year on condition that all children under a certain age were admitted, and a basket was hung at the gate for unwanted children.

The Foundling Hospital was renowned for its pictures and for the chapel services to which hundreds of people flocked to hear the singing of the children. Handel was a frequent visitor and benefactor, and Londoners heard his 'Messiah' at the Foundling Hospital after its first performance in Dublin.

Even in early years it was customary to board out children under five years of age with foster mothers in the country. Some came to Berkhamsted and did not benefit from the country air; no fewer than eleven foundlings died here in 1759–60. A little information about the education of the children is contained in the following letter dated 1767, from Mrs. Jeffreys, wife of the rector of Berkhamsted, to the secretary to the Foundling Hospital:

Sir,—I intend sending Mary Johnson up to the Hospital next Thursday by the Waggon. I have today had information of her having got the Itch. I therefore give you notice of her coming that care may be taken of her. The girl takes on sadly at leaving her Nurse, that I hope she will be us'd with tenderness, tho' she has that disagreeable distemper.

I have inclosed patterns of the Lace the Children make, there is no other employment for them at this place, the Nurses teach them to Read and say their Catechism, but most of them are backward in Reading, and it cannot be expected that common Nurses are capable of teaching them well.

In 1926 the valuable estate of the Foundling Hospital in London was sold and the children were sent to temporary premises in Redhill until 1935, when the Georgian-style buildings at Berkhamsted were ready for occupation. They were designed to accommodate 400 children between five and fifteen years of age, with the chapel as the great central feature.

For some time the children continued to wear the traditional uniform: the boys in brown Eton jackets and trousers with scarlet waistcoats, brass buttons, starched collars and black bows; the girls in brown serge tunics with white linen caps, tippets and aprons. It was a stirring sight when the boys and girls, headed by their band, marched down Chesham Road and Castle Street to the railway station to start their annual holiday.

The costume was abandoned during the 1939–45 war and important changes in the administration of the charity were made. The name was changed to the Thomas Coram Foundation.

In 1951 a secondary modern school was established for town as well as Coram children of eleven years and upwards. The Hertfordshire County Council purchased the buildings and forty acres of playing fields from the Thomas Coram Foundation in 1955. All the Coram children left to be boarded out, and in September 1955 the grammar school stream was added, making Ashlyns the first bi-lateral school in Hertfordshire. The domestic accommodation was converted into classrooms, science laboratories, domestic science rooms, craft rooms, etc. The first headmaster of the bi-lateral school, Mr. J. H. Babington, G.C., was succeeded by Mr. A. N. Johnston in 1972, when Ashlyns, now an Upper school, received its first intake of 13 years old children under the three-tier system mentioned later in this chapter.

The Bourne School

One of the town's most generous benefactors was Thomas Bourne (1656–1729), who bequeathed £8,000 to build and endow a charity school for twenty boys and ten girls. Taking into account the change in the value of money, it was a remarkable bounty. No less remarkable was the slender link between the donor and Berkhamsted. Bourne was not even a resident of the town, though he came here occasionally to visit his sister, Sarah Rolfe. Like Thomas Coram, Bourne was one of many rich men of the period who founded schools or hospitals for poor children, and he doubtless favoured Berkhamsted because Camberwell, where he lived, already had a charity school.

After making generous provision for his relatives, he left £3,000 to the Framework Knitters' Company, of which he was Master, for erecting an almshouse in London, and £8,000 for a 'free school in West Berkhamstead'. This rare name was used to distinguish the town from Little Berkhamsted, in east Hertfordshire.

The executors wasted so much time before carrying out Bourne's directions that the rector, the Rev. John Cowper, took legal proceedings against them. In 1735 the Attorney General ordered payment of the money, and thanks to wise investment the sum of £8,000 had grown to over £9,000 in six years. In accordance with the will, £700 was spent on building a school and apartments for the master and mistress, who lived there rent-free and received stipends of £30 and £15 a year respectively. Increases were not granted for many years. Not surprisingly, some teachers exercised their right to take in paying pupils.

The first master and mistress, Edward and Elizabeth Eastmead, started their duties in 1737. Free uniforms were supplied to the boys and girls, and their parents received 1*s*. or 1*s*. 6*d*. a week, as funds permitted. £24 was set aside each year for boys who were apprenticed on leaving school. Bourne's birthday, December 16, was to be commemorated by the distribution of £5 to the poor and by a sermon preached in St. Peter's Church, mentioning his charities. The will also directed the trustees to pay £5 per annum to the Greencoat School at Camberwell.

School hours were from 7 to 11 a.m. and 1 to 5 p.m. in summer, from 8 to 11 a.m. and 1 to 4 p.m. in winter. A week at Easter and Whitsun, four weeks at harvest time, and fifteen days at Christmas were the only 'play days' allowed. There was a list of 'crimes' for which children were to be expelled, and penalties were no less severe for the master and mistress if they showed incapacity or neglect, indulged in 'extream' severity towards any of the children, or lacked sobriety. Not that any objection was raised to the building of a brewhouse at the bottom of the school garden in 1756, despite the fact that a long-forgotten alehouse, the Wheatsheaf, adjoined the school.

Bourne directed that the boys were to be taught to 'read English, write and cast accounts,' while the girls, 'after being perfected in reading English,' were to 'do such work as the churchwardens should think fit for such girls to learn.' Not until 1761 were the girls taught to write as well as read, and then only in their last year at school.

The trustees deliberated for months before agreeing that it was 'very decent and proper' to accede to the master's request that the children be taught to sing psalms.

'Girl comes lousy to school, month's pay and expulsion threatened,' reported the clerk in 1757. Afterwards, not being 'clean and free from vermine,' she was expelled. Some years later, the children (among whom was William Shakespeare, destined to rise to the rank of parish constable) were warned that they would have to pay for the repair of any windows they broke.

For two years the weekly payments to scholars' parents were not made, and some of them borrowed money, sure that in due course they would be paid, but one unfortunate father was sent to Hertford for debt.

At Easter, each boy, in accordance with Bourne's detailed instructions, received a kersey coat, woollen waistcoat, leather breeches, woollen cap, two linen bands, two shirts, two pairs of shoes, and two pairs of woollen stockings. Each girl received a grey woollen gown and petticoat, a flannel under-petticoat, two linen shifts, two blue and white aprons, two linen bands, two pairs of shoes, two pairs of stockings, and 'one pair of boddice.' Bourne intended that £75 should be set aside each year for clothes, but for many years the cost varied between £42 and £50.

In 1853, public subscriptions were invited for the provision of a new classroom behind the original building. The cost was £391, of which £200 was subscribed by General John Finch, of Berkhamsted Place. A year later the General defrayed the entire cost of rebuilding the original school building, which was in a dilapidated state.

But the years of the Bourne School as a separate institution were numbered. In 1875, all the boys and girls were transferred to the National School (p. 54), and the traditional uniform was discontinued, though distinctive bonnets and caps were worn until 1914, when an annual dinner to the scholars was also stopped. Only minor provisions of the will, such as the annual sermon and the gift to Camberwell, were retained, the most important new departure being the creation of scholarships worth £5 per annum for a limited number of boys and girls attending Church of England schools. If they passed a simple examination, they became the new 'Bourne scholars.'

In 1949, the trustees, with the consent of the Charity Commissioners, appointed no more 'scholars' but increased the number of grants or exhibitions to boys and girls attending grammar schools or other places of secondary or further education or training.

To perpetuate the benefactor's name, a Middle school, opened in

1971, was called the Thomas Bourne School. His coat of arms (with the arms of the town and of General Finch) is above the door of the old charity school building, 222 High Street.

Other Schools

In 1830, nine-tenths of the children of Berkhamsted and Northchurch received no schooling whatever on weekdays. The grammar school was moribund, the Bourne School was limited to thirty scholars, and a few small private schools, grandly called academies, were beyond the means of most of the inhabitants.

Many boys and girls, however, were taught to read and write at Sunday schools. The first was established in June 1810 by Joseph Hobbs, pastor of the Baptist church, with the support of the Congregational minister. A few months later, the Church of England provided Sunday schools in Berkhamsted and Northchurch.

A great step forward was taken in March 1833, when the vestry unanimously supported Augustus Smith's resolution 'that a good parish school should be established, where both boys and girls should be taught reading, writing and arithmetic, and useful work.' What was known as the British school, for boys and girls of all religious denominations, was opened at the corner of Park View Road in July 1834.

A National (Church of England) elementary school followed exactly four years later. Classrooms and a house for the master were built beside and behind the Court House. The first annual report, dated 1839, shows that 238 children were admitted: 136 boys, of whom about 100 attended regularly, and 102 girls, of whom an average of 50 attended regularly. The Church of England continued to take the initiative, building an infants' school at Gossoms End in 1844, a mixed school at Potten End in 1856, and a mixed school at Northchurch in 1864. The Court House school was enlarged, an infants' department was provided in Chapel Street, and a separate boys' school (for Northchurch) was built at Gossoms End.

Before compulsory education was introduced, attendance figures were deplorably low. The rector, the Rev. John Cobb, complained in 1874 about the practice of sending children for half a day only. Absenteeism was often due to the parents' inability to find the 'school pence,' in other words the penny, twopence or threepence they were required to pay for their children's education. A Government grant was available, but it was not to exceed the aggregate amount of school pence and voluntary subscriptions, and was withheld if children attended less than 250 times a year.

In 1875, 453 children attended the National school and 292 the

Board (formerly the British) school, the annual cost of educating each child being £1 4s. 1d. and £1 9s. 6d. respectively. First prize for good attendance was won by a girl who attended 417 times. The fifteenth girl on the list went to school only 205 times, but nevertheless won a prize for good attendance.

The School Board, formed in 1871, enlarged the school at Park View Road corner and provided a separate department for infants in 1894. There was no room for expansion on the Court House site; in 1897 the Church of England built the first Victoria school (for boys) in Prince Edward Street, and when a girls' school was built next door a few years later, all the classrooms in Back Lane were vacated.

Shortly before the 1939–45 war, official approval was given to a Church of England proposal to build a Secondary school at Greenway; this scheme was abandoned when local children were admitted to Ashlyns School.

In 1970 the decision was taken to adopt a three-tier system of comprehensive education with seven First schools taking pupils from five to nine years of age (Victoria, Westfield, Greenway, St. Thomas More, Swing Gate, Northchurch, Potten End); three Middle schools for pupils from nine to 13 (Augustus Smith, Thomas Bourne and Bridgewater); and one Upper school, Ashlyns, for pupils from 13 to 18.

Evening classes for men and women were available as early as 1843 at the Court House, the heaviest expenditure being on coal, oil, copy books at 3d. each and pens at a little over a halfpenny each. The Mechanics' Institute provided many evening classes in Victorian times, and in 1892 the Northchurch Technical Institute started holding woodwork classes in a barn at Durrants Farm and drawing classes in the village school. Technical education was then assisted by means of a direct tax on whisky; the sale of every bottle helped young men to quench a thirst for knowledge and skill, and the Northchurch Institute received a particularly large grant when the tax was wound up. The Co-operative Society, with a very active education committee, also provided evening classes. According to Loosley's directory for 1909, classes were held nearly every evening at the Town Hall, Council school, a coffee tavern in Castle Street and Mr. Osborn's yard in Park Street.

Between the wars the premises opposite the Town Hall, now the Berkhamsted annexe of the Dacorum College of Further Education, became an evening school, largely through the efforts of Philip Brandon-Jones, an art master at Berkhamsted School, and with much financial help from Miss Sidney Courtauld, a member of the famous family of textile manufacturers.

VI
From Borough to Urban Council

A FAMILIAR REMINDER of the former Corporation of Berkhamsted is the coat of arms which was granted to the bailiff and capital burgesses over 350 years ago. The design was chosen 'upon deliberate consideration that the glory of that place hath proceeded from the ancient castle there... In a shield, or, a triple tow'red castle azure, within a border of Cornewall, viz., sables besanted.'

Little glory, however, proceeded from James I's grant of a full charter of incorporation in 1618. The Corporation derived no lasting benefits from its privileges, and ceased to exist by 1662-3. A local historian may be pardoned for wishing that it had continued to the present day, not for the pomp and circumstance, but for the very strong possibility that the borough records would have shed much light on the character as well as the activities of the mayors and aldermen. A council chamber tends to generate more heat than a vestry.

Two years before Berkhamsted received the charter of 1618, Sir John Norden conducted a survey and was told that 'Barkhamsted is an ancient Borough and Market Town and very likely has been a Corporation, and time out of memory of man always reputed to be a borough...' Domesday Book (1086) mentions 52 burgesses, and there is a reference to Saxon and Norman privileges in the town's first-known charter, granted at Oxford in 1156 by Henry II, who promised the men and merchants of Berkhamsted that they were to enjoy 'as well and as honourably, and better and more honourably,' the laws and customs which they had in the days of Edward the Confessor, William I and Henry I. The charter further declared that wherever they went with their merchandise throughout England, Normandy, Aquitaine and Anjou, the men and merchants were to be quit of all tolls and duties; anyone disquieting them was to forfeit £10.

Henry III confirmed his grandfather's charter, and Edward IV, in 1447, additionally directed that no market was to be set up within eleven miles of the town and that Berkhamsted men were not to be summoned for jury service. The latter right was cited successfully at Hertford as late as 1840, but many ancient privileges of this kind were abolished by Act of Parliament in 1870.

The charters were confirmed by Richard III in 1484 and by Elizabeth I in 1598.

The Corporation

The town's last charter, dated July 18, 1618, is thought to have been granted by James I as a reward or bribe to the townspeople for not opposing the enclosure of a portion of the Common (p. 94).

Berkhamsted was created a free borough town, the inhabitants to be 'one body corporate and politic.' The charter stated that the first bailiff was to be Francis Barker, who lived at Pilkington Manor House, on the site of the shops and flats opposite Rectory Lane. Twelve capital burgesses, with the bailiff, were to constitute the common council and serve for life or as long as they were of good behaviour. Each year the capital burgesses were to elect the bailiff, recorder, clerk, and two sergeants at the mace. The Corporation was permitted to have 'a certain counsell-house or guild-hall,' make bye-laws for the borough, impose fines, penalties and imprisonments, maintain a 'prison or goale' [sic], collect market tolls and rents of stalls, have an extra market day each week and two additional fair days annually, hold a court of record once a month, a court of the market to deal with petty offences occurring on market days, and a court of pied poudre (Old French for dusty feet) to give speedy justice while the dust of the fairground was still falling from the feet of pedlars and others involved in disputes.

Thus the Corporation was closely connected with the everyday life of the town, especially the markets and fairs. Unfortunately, the first record book cannot be traced; perhaps it was more informative than the one for 1637–62, which is in the church chest. After 1641 little was recorded beyond the election of officers. Looking like a cheap exercise book, it seems to symbolise the poverty of the Corporation; the Vestry, the rating authority, could afford a handsomely bound tome.

'Let none deride or evil do or speak against the Corporation, the Bailiff, or any of the Capital Burgesses.' So ran the first of the 'orders and constitutions.' Penalties were to be imposed upon burgesses who did not attend meetings, left before meetings were over, refused to give opinions, or revealed 'any thinge of the Corporation to the scandall, damage or injury thereof, or of any of the members or officers thereof.'

No person was to let a house within the borough to a stranger or allow any person to stay in his house for more than a month without giving 'such security to save the parish harmes from all charges and troubles.' If any stranger wished to become an inhabitant, he was to 'compound for his freedom and pay five pounds at the least before he sette up or useth any manner of trade there.' Another order, one of the last made by the Corporation, limited the number of alehouses to six.

An inventory of 1642 mentions the charter, the mace, the common seal with a silver head, the arms of the borough, a table with a frame, a green carpet and twelve cushions, three books, the standard weights and measures, three seals 'to seale measures,' a holdfast and hammer, two pairs of handcuffs and a shackle.

The Corporation, empowered to maintain a prison, inherited a small lock-up or cage for the detention of petty offenders, mentioned in a document of 1616. Later, the borough provided a Bridewell or house of correction for the Dacorum Hundred, which contributed £30 to 'erect and furnish' the house. The bailiff and chief burgesses, however, converted and furnished an existing house. In 1639, when Hemel Hempstead provided a Bridewell for the Hundred, its Berkhamsted counterpart was sold, allegedly to the profit of the borough. The burgesses were in disgrace for not returning the £30 received from the Hundred; a claim by the bailiff that £30 and more had been spent on converting and furnishing the house was not well received at the Hoddesdon sessions.

Having lost a Bridewell, the Corporation decided, in 1640, to build a new 'jayle,' comprising a cell $7\frac{1}{2}$ feet square and 'one roome over the same.' The estimated price of £6 10*s.* was to include labour and all materials except locks. Later, a larger scheme was favoured, and Thomas Piddleton, a carpenter, contracted to build a lock-up 12 feet long and 8 feet broad. The price went up to £12.

Besides discussing common rights and other weighty questions, the chief burgesses listened to minor complaints. 'Upon displeasure only and without any other juste cause,' Nicholas Moores turned his servant, Joan Brookes, out of his house four years before her contract had expired and detained some of her clothing. The record book continues, 'Wee upon full hearinge of all parties have thought it best to dissolve the said contracte, ordering and commandinge the said Moores to delivver all apparel the said Joan did bring with hir ... one linsey woolsey apron, one pare of shoes, one blacke hatte, two wollen wastcoates.'

In 1639, one of the chief burgesses, Robert Newman, son of the rector, 'made relation of the answere from the merchante with whom he formerlye had conferred about sendynge some of the boyes beyond the seas to some of the American Ilandes: viz. that he will take a dozen if we will clothe them or gyve the merchante 20*s.* apiece and he will clothe them himself. And requires to know how many wee will send unto hym and gyve hym notice thereof in due tyme.' There is no further reference to this subject.

Robert Darvell, threatened with a £5 fine for refusing to become a capital burgess, emigrated to America. He was one of a number of men who refused or were reluctant to take office. It seems that only men of substance could afford to be capital burgesses; they had to pay for the privilege, and in 1639, when there was some question of renewing the charter, every capital burgess was expected to pay '5£ a peece towardes the charge of it.' When a dinner was held in 1628, it was ordered that 'every burghesse doo pay yeerely 4s.'

Those who continued to serve during the Civil War and Commonwealth knew how little was the power behind the glory of being a bailiff or capital burgess. The Corporation controlled a very small area and revenues were correspondingly small. The market declined until the tolls were negligible. Then, in 1661–2, two successive bailiffs died during their terms of office, a serious loss for an ailing council. The last bailiff, Christopher Woodhouse, a surgeon, presided over a dying body; during his term of office the Corporation ceased to exist.

A few townspeople, knowing the weaknesses of the old Corporation, had sufficient enthusiasm to appeal to Charles II for a new charter in 1664, suggesting an extension of the boundary to include Northchurch and the changing of market day from Thursday to Friday, obviously because Hemel Hempstead market, held on Thursday, was taking all the trade.

Nothing came of the appeal, and it may be assumed that the borough's anti-Royalist attitude before and during the Civil War was not unknown in Whitehall. Had the Corporation been revived with the addition of Northchurch, it might have prospered, but the villagers had no cause to love their neighbours (p. 94). As late as 1935 some residents of Northchurch resented the inclusion of the village in the urban district.

Towns smaller than Berkhamsted—Wallingford, for instance, which shared our early charters—are still boroughs, but only because they guarded and cherished ancient rights. In Victorian times a surgeon, Thomas Whately, started a campaign for a charter, and in his time there may still have been some chance of success, but he died suddenly and none of his supporters pursued the matter.

Manorial Courts

The Corporation's meetings were held in an Elizabethan hall which still survives. Early documents refer to it as the church house or town hall, but for generations it has been called the Court House, taking its name from the manorial and borough courts which were held within its walls. The row of shops in front of Back Lane has robbed the Court House of its former prominence, and the lower part has been refaced with brick and flint, but the projecting upper chamber is original, and beneath the timbered roof, exposed when the 'great loft' was removed, much of the town's business was discussed.

The oldest court of all, the View of Frankpledge, probably originated in the earliest days of the Dacorum Hundred, to which Berkhamsted belongs. This and other courts were held at the castle, or, in times of sickness, at an oak within the park or a willow outside the park. Matters dealt with included the transfer of land, fines payable to the lord of the manor on the death of a tenant, debts, breaches of contract, poaching and other offences, highway obstructions and other nuisances, the selling of food and drink of poor quality or at too high a price, and the appointment of officers of the manor. Once a year, in October, the constables, vice-constables, flesh-tasters, bread-tasters, beer-tasters and water bailiffs were nominated, a custom which continued at the Court House until mid-Victorian times. Latterly, to the bitter regret of the ale-taster, there were no duties to perform.

The Vestry

For much of its long life the Vestry was a powerful local governing body, having control over many matters that are now in the hands of several authorities. It was the Vestry which relieved the poor, maintained a workhouse, started schools and provided a pest-house, a very necessary institution when small-pox, cholera and other diseases were rife. The provision of a fire service was the duty of the parish, the engine being kept in St. Peter's Church. The parish was also responsible for maintaining law and order, though the constables were nominated at the manorial court, not at the annual Vestry meeting. Thus the Vestry was concerned with every aspect of local government, but so many economic and social changes have taken place that it would be unrealistic to compare its rather rough and ready methods with those of a modern council.

All owners of houses and lands had a right to participate in parochial business, a right which was accompanied by the duty to serve as churchwardens, overseers of the poor, surveyors of highways, and constables.

Churchwardens were originally concerned with the maintenance and repair of the church fabric, but in later times many duties, non-ecclesiastical as well as ecclesiastical, were thrust upon them.

Stonewardens or surveyors of highways were required by the Highway Act of 1555 to maintain roads by the old principle of unpaid service by local men; they were able to levy a highway rate in addition to the imposition of statute labour.

A SHORT HISTORY OF BERKHAMSTED

Overseers of the poor were the hardest-worked officers of all. The famous Poor Law Act of 1601 ordered every parish to set people to work who had 'no ordinary trade to get their living by', the overseers being empowered to levy rates to provide materials and equipment, to relieve lame, blind and impotent persons, to put out children as apprentices, and, for the impotent poor only, to build poorhouses. Having to maintain its own poor, every parish tried to stop poor persons coming in from other parishes and becoming chargeable on the rates. Labouring men were virtually prisoners in their own parish unless they could afford to become tenants of houses and land worth £10 a year.

It was never easy to provide work for the poor. James I gave £100 to Berkhamsted 'to set the poor to work in a manufactory,' but the churchwardens took an easy way out by purchasing land with the money and using the rent to aid the poor rate, a misapplication which benefited the ratepayers instead of the poor until 1757, when the Vestry agreed to use the rent to buy bread for the poor.

Charles I also gave £100 for the poor of Berkhamsted, specifying that they were to be employed in Jersey, but something went wrong with the scheme. Only £82 of the £100 was recovered, and with this sum the churchwardens bought a row of tenements called Ragged Row. Here paupers were given rent-free homes by the overseers, thereby preserving some semblance of family life instead of going to the workhouse. A house which actually adjoined St. Peter's Church at the south-west corner was also given to a pauper family.

One of the greatest indignities ever inflicted upon the poor was an order that every person receiving poor relief was to wear 'upon the shoulder of the right sleeve of his upper or uppermost garment a large Roman letter P with the first letter of the name of the parish cut in red or blue cloth.' Many poor people in Berkhamsted bore the badge 'P.B.'

The Workhouse

In the eighteenth and early nineteenth century the workhouse was a wretched, straw-thatched building on land that was afterwards occupied by Park View School. The workhouse master's accounts remind one of the evils described by Dickens, yet now and again an item reveals a little act of kindness, such as the gift, in 1727, of an ounce and a half of tobacco, costing twopence, to an inmate named Mary Ross. Jane Hall's boy was given 'a point of ale,' $1\frac{1}{2}d$., and Jane Ward's boy received 'half a point,' $\frac{3}{4}d$. George Hoare, whose name also appears as a keeper of the Bridewell, was appointed governor of the workhouse in 1767 at £28 per calendar month; he was also permitted to have the proceeds of the 'work, labour and service' of the poor in his charge. But he had to clothe and feed the inmates, pay for their medicines, and undertake to 'deliver up the poor to the parish officers in good condition'—a very necessary clause, though scarcely sufficient to exclude exploitation of the poor and abuse of public money. New governors were appointed at frequent intervals.

In 1777, the churchwardens ordered the governor to 'bring or cause to be brought twice every Sunday to church all the men, women and children that are able.' In 1796, probably because the cost was too high, the churchwardens declined a sea captain's offer to take unwanted boys to America at £5 a head. In the same year, Thomas Dorrien and James Croft, the overseers, made it known that not more than six children were to be apprenticed to each chimney sweep; the period of apprenticeship was eight to 15 years, by which time the boys were presumably too big to climb up chimneys.

The worst period in the history of poor law came after the Napoleonic wars. Many farmers, immediately after the harvest, discharged most of their men and advised them to apply to the overseers, who were bound to find the men employment or relieve them if there was no parish work to be done. As a rule overseers asked the farmers to continue employing the men at reduced wages, the deficiency being made up from the rates. Thus honest men were pauperised against their will, and ever-increasing rates placed such a heavy burden on poorer ratepayers that many had to be excused payment.

In 1824, when so many paupers were employed on road repairs that the offices of overseers of the poor and highway surveyors were combined, the Berkhamsted Vestry invited the Northchurch Vestry to unite for purposes of poor law administration. It was proposed to build a workhouse to serve both parishes, but Northchurch was at first reluctant to part with its own workhouse.

Both the poor and the ratepayers were helped by the Rev. George Nugent, who, though rector of Bygrave, near Baldock, spent most of his time at the Red House, Berkhamsted. More than anyone else he was moved to pity by the plight of the workhouse inmates. He died in 1830 and bequeathed £1,000 for a new workhouse, which was built at the corner of Kitsbury Road, replacing Ragged Row.

By 1832 some Northchurch parishioners doubted the wisdom of maintaining a separate workhouse. A parish meeting decided to transfer the inmates to Berkhamsted, and the Northchurch workhouse, near Billet Lane corner, was closed. At last town and village had a common interest, the workhouse, but in 1834 further centralisation was enforced by the setting up of boards of guardians to administer poor law in groups of parishes, known as unions. Thus the new workhouse, originally intended for the poor of Berkhamsted alone, had to serve several parishes. It was used until 1935, when all the inmates were transferred to Hemel Hempstead. Nugent House, as it was called when the use of the word 'workhouse' was discouraged, was sold for £3,700, and down came bricks and an inscribed stone which proclaimed George Nugent's 'munificent gift.'

The Bridewell

Unlike the workhouse, which was maintained by the parish, the Bridewell, or prison, was the responsibility of the justices. As already mentioned, a Bridewell existed in Berkhamsted in the days of the Corporation, but subsequently the prisoners were sent to Hemel Hempstead. Then, in 1764, Berkhamsted again had a Bridewell. T. H. Noyes was instructed to find a suitable place for it, and like the Corporation over a century earlier, he favoured converting existing property, selecting a row of small tenements at the corner of Cocks Lane, afterwards called Bridewell Lane and now known as King's Road. The purchase price was £112, and after alterations had been completed at a cost of £120 12*s*. 10*d*., Berkhamsted acquired a new Bridewell on what is now one of the most valuable sites in the town.

The first keeper, George Hoare, received a salary of £20 a year; he died four years later and Sarah Hoare was appointed keeper at the same salary as her late husband. For nursing a prisoner suffering from small-pox she received £5 8*s*. 9*d*.

By 1779 the justices must have wished that Mr. Noyes had built a brand new Bridewell. The converted tenements were 'insufficient for the safe custody of persons committed thereto' and such repairs as were carried out did not prevent prisoners escaping. Thomas Wildly, sentenced to twelve months' imprisonment for petty larceny in 1784, lived up to his name; he was put in irons but nevertheless forced a way through the thin wall dividing the cell from John Dorrien's stable. He was recaptured at Northampton. Three years later, John Ghost was publicly whipped and imprisoned for leaving his family chargeable to the parish of Tring. He, too, broke out of gaol, was recaptured, and sentenced to another public whipping and six months' imprisonment.

A Berkhamsted carpenter named Loader was paid £33 to strengthen the Bridewell, but determined and desperate men still broke out.

In 1782, in accordance with the requirements of a new Act of Parliament, the rector (the Rev. John Jeffreys), the Rev. Walter Bingham and Thomas Halsey were appointed to inspect the Bridewell. They found two men who were 'almost naked'; four shirts were ordered for them at a cost of 10*d*. each.

At the Midsummer Sessions, 1789, a committee of justices reported that the Bridewell was still insecure: 'The rooms for men and women want air. The men's prison is 16½ feet by 10½ feet, the women's 17 feet by 11 feet ... It is but very indifferently watered; no employment, no furniture. Keeper's salary £20. Prisoner's allowance 1 lb. of bread per day and water, and let out once a day. One side of this prison is against a cooper's shop, and that partition is a mud wall raddled, and inside of the prison lined with an inch board. They can converse. There is a dungeon, a most dreadful hole, without air, without any light, nine steps down and the brick bottom perished. In future no prisoner is to be put into this place. The average number committed here in a year is about 14.'

In 1792, W. Rogers, the keeper, was granted an additional £8 per annum for prisoners' bread allowance, and in the same year a special allowance of £3 13s. 6d. was made for bread and straw for the prisoners.

By the 1820s it was generally agreed that the Bridewell had outlived its usefulness, and on at least two occasions the justices all but decided to sell the property. Finally, in 1843, alterations costing £56 10s. were made to 'render the place fit for a police station to which prisoners might be remanded before commitment, but it would not be fit for prisoners under any sentence, however short.'

For all its internal horrors, the Bridewell had the appearance from the High Street of a pleasant double-fronted house. An overhanging storey kept rain off the constables as they stood outside the door in King's Road. But the road was very narrow, and when the old building and an adjoining shop were pulled down in 1894, part of the site was sacrificed to widen the road. The police station of late Victorian times was demolished in 1972, to be replaced by a new station.

The Sanitary Authority

Returning to the Vestry, which gradually lost its non-ecclesiastical duties in the nineteenth century, it is interesting to note how private donations and public subscriptions enabled the town to acquire new buildings and services at no cost to the ratepayers. In 1788, the cost of a new fire engine, £58 15s., was over-subscribed by £6. In 1849, the townspeople gave £106 for the first street lamps and piping; the Vestry merely had to pay for the gas and maintenance out of the rates. Several schools, the Town Hall, and a new road to the railway station, Lower King's Road, did not cost the ratepayers a penny.

Rural sanitary authorities were formed in 1872, creating extra work for the guardians, who, after each meeting devoted to the relief of the poor, held a second meeting to deal with public health matters.

The old police station (*above*) and King's Road before it was widened in late Victorian times

Above: Castle Street, *c.* 1860

Below: Another view *c.* 1900 showing the 'sunken' cottages (p. 85)

The Berkhamsted Union and Rural Sanitary Authority, as it was called, was in charge of several parishes with a total population of 15,090 and a rateable value of £91,076 in 1881. Its first major achievement was the building of Aldbury isolation hospital, such a great improvement on the old type of pest house that the plans were borrowed by several other sanitary authorities. The Berkhamsted pest house, now a private house, still stands on the Common; no patients have been received there for over a century.

Few people would talk about the 'good old days' if they knew more about the filth, the diseases, the stinks and the many discomforts and nuisances that were rife until Victorian times. Street cleansing was always inadequate. The unpaid highway surveyors for ever fought a losing battle in the days of unmetalled roads, unpaved footpaths, horse-drawn traffic and constant processions of cattle and sheep on the way to market. There was another hazard, indicated by a warning from the Vestry in 1824 that women who threw slops out of bedroom windows would be prosecuted.

Nash says that all kinds of vegetable refuse were cast into the street. Pigs were the recognised scavengers. The rainfall took its own course and found its own level, 'sometimes resting in large pools in front of dwellings, waiting for the sun to evaporate it, and in the meantime providing a cooling bath for pigs to wallow in. On private property cesspits were the only method of dealing with sewage, and it was no uncommon thing to see on the south side of the street the drainage from manure heaps flowing from the several gateways.'

A 'black ditch' in the valley—an open sewer—caused the *Berkhamsted Times* to protest in 1875 that 'the inhabitants in mid-town had for years inhaled the reeking breath of the Castle Street stream.' Three years later a London firm prepared a sewerage scheme, and on hearing that the works would cost £6,300, plus land and other expenses of £6,000, Captain Hamilton, of Highfield House, said that no one outside Bedlam would think of spending that sum on 'a useless and dangerous experiment.' So-called economists were still protesting in 1892, when the Rural Sanitary Authority approved a scheme which, at a public meeting, was condemned as being excessive and extravagant. Unfortunately, forecasts that money was being poured down the drain were correct; the system was defective.

The Urban District Council

The Local Government Act of 1888 transferred the local functions of justices of the peace to newly-founded county councils and county boroughs, and in 1894 another Act distributed the work in urban areas between borough and urban district councils. In 1894 the Rural

Sanitary Authority became the Rural District Council, but the Berkhamsted Urban District Council did not come into being until 1898. At the first election, sixteen candidates contested the twelve seats. Mr. David Osborn headed the poll with 346 votes; 169 were sufficient to elect the twelfth man, Mr. William Chilton.

Having no civic centre, no full time officials, not even an office to call its own, the Council met fortnightly at the workhouse. Mr. Thomas Penny, solicitor, was appointed clerk at £50 per annum. Mr. E. H. Adey, who also worked for other local authorities, received £75 from Berkhamsted as inspector of nuisances, £2 as inspector of dairies and cowsheds, £3 as inspector of canal boats, and £20 as surveyor.

The council inherited a faulty drainage and sewerage system on which the Rural Sanitary Authority had already spent £13,812. That sum, it was stated, was practically lost, 'just as if it had been cast into the sea', and much of the work had to be reconstructed. It was a time of high spending and great inconvenience; the relaying of pipes ruined paths and roads, sarcastic comments appeared in the local papers, and some of the councillors wondered whether they were in their right minds to seek election. Complaints of extravagant spending led to the formation of a ratepayers' association, and it was not long before the councillors themselves made the first of many protests about the County Council's 'enormous and ever increasing expenditure.' For a quiet time, the Vestry, now concerned only with ecclesiastical matters, was much to be preferred; only six people, other than reporters, turned up for the annual meeting in 1899. Northchurch, being outside the urban district, had a parish council, and 120 electors attended the first annual meeting.

When the urban district was formed the appalling mistake was made of excluding George Street, Ellesmere Road and several smaller roads, which, being in the detached portion of the parish of St. Mary, remained under the somewhat remote control of Northchurch Parish Council. In 1909, however, Sunnyside was transferred to the urban district, increasing its acreage from 1,035 to 1,208. The number of councillors was raised from twelve to fifteen, and three more were added when a large part of the village of Northchurch was transferred to the urban district in 1935, increasing the acreage to 1,982. Until that time town and village had joint committees to deal with sewerage and fire brigade matters.

Berkhamsted Urban District Council was one of the first small authorities in the country to take an interest in town planning. Unfortunately, it was the townspeople's apathy which killed a scheme which, shortly after the 1914–18 war, would have transformed the area between the railway station and the High Street. A war memorial committee, formed with the backing of the Council, made the following recommendations:

1. Extension of the Moor to include the whole area between the canal, Mill Street, Lower King's Road and what is now called Greene Field road.
2. Erection of a war memorial on the extended recreation ground, possibly taking the form of a bridge over the Bulbourne.
3. Demolition of the old brewery (now occupied by shops and part of the car park on the west side of Water Lane), to be used for public buildings.
4. Demolition of the slum area between the Wilderness and Water Lane, leaving an open space.
5. Acquisition and demolition of the brewery stores, stables and Adelbert House, the sites to be added to the recreation ground, and preservation of the wharf near the station as an open space.

Mr. Edward Greene, of The Hall, was prepared to give the brewery site, Earl Brownlow was ready to grant a 999 years' lease of the meadow adjoining the Moor, Mr. and Mrs. Berlein, of Cross Oak, offered to provide an infants' welfare centre in Water Lane in memory of two sons killed in the war, Sir Richard Cooper wished to build a technical school or some other memorial to his father, Mr. David Pike offered to buy and present the old Baptist burial ground for use as an open space in memory of a son killed in the war, and the Urban Council was willing to purchase and demolish slum property in the Wilderness.

With offers from five donors worth many thousands of pounds and the Council's offer of support up to a penny rate, the committee appealed to the townspeople for £9,000 to complete the scheme. So poor was the response that the committee could only proceed with the erection of the war memorial which now stands in St. Peter's churchyard. A scheme of permanent value, which today would cost many hundreds of thousands of pounds, was irretrievably lost.

The Council could have taken a stronger line and offered a larger contribution, but here, as in many other towns, golden opportunities were lost to 'save the rates.' The widening of the railway bridge near the station and improvements to pathless roads could have been undertaken at very reasonable cost, but so-called economists had the loudest voices. Until the late 1920s Berkhamsted still had a horse-drawn fire engine!

On the credit side, housing problems have been tackled with vigour; the Council's greatest achievement was the building of 1,300 houses by 1972. Its own house, the Civic Centre, was designed by a former town surveyor, the late Mr. J. R. Hadfield, and opened in 1938, a distinct improvement on the workhouse boardroom in which the Council held its first meeting in 1898

VII
Industries and Crafts

For many centuries Berkhamsted was self-sufficient apart from salt, millstones, iron and such novelties as were introduced by itinerant traders. Food, drink, fuel, clothing, utensils, implements, building materials—all were grown, found or made in the district.

The Saxon farmers who cleared scrub and forest built their own houses and made everything they used. Some men, of course, were better at one task or another than their neighbours: as the settlement grew, some became craftsmen and merchants. If the makers of platters, ladles, bowls and farm implements are singled out, it is because Berkhamsted has always made good use of its timber; until the early years of this century small articles of wood were manufactured in great variety and volume.

Builders, too, never lacked timber, neither were they ever short of flints for building the castle, churches and houses. When they started using bricks, ample deposits of clay were found where gorse and wood were available for firing the kilns. It was only when stone was specified that man and beast had to struggle over hilly tracks from Bedfordshire with Totternhoe stone.

Of course, agriculture has always been the most essential industry of all. London received much of its grain from Hertfordshire, and the high quality of the wheat was said to be due in part to the unlimited supplies of manure that the waggoners were able to bring back from the streets and stables of London. But there were years when yields were low and prices were high; the agricultural labourer was often the first to suffer. The Berkhamsted churchwardens, in pious despair, attributed a bad harvest to 'the heavy Hand of God.'

In the nineteenth century, wheat was valued not for the grain alone but for high-quality straw that was especially suitable for plaiting. Generations of cottagers were able to earn money at home, plaiting straw for Bedfordshire hat-makers.

Barley, too, has always been an important crop. According to Norden, in Elizabethan times the principal industry in Berkhamsted was the manufacture of malt; this, however, was a very widespread industry, found in every town and large village until it passed into the hands of large manufacturers.

A minor point of interest is John Cobb's claim that red clover and swede turnips were grown for the first time in England at Broadway Farm, between Berkhamsted and Bourne End.

In this traditionally arable district, livestock played a secondary role, but sheep added to the prosperity of Berkhamsted in both ancient and modern times. The wool trade was so considerable in the thirteenth and fourteenth centuries that several local merchants had agencies in Flanders. In Victorian times sheep were the foundation of a great Berkhamsted business, for William Cooper's highly effective sheep dip was the first of many products which are known all over the world.

The Wool Merchants

In May 1332, Edward III sent a letter to English wool merchants at Bruges; among them were four Berkhamsted men, John le Fuller, Ralph de Cheddington, William le Shepard, and John Gentilcorps; the last-named was probably a brother of Thomas Gentilcorps, one of three men who represented Berkhamsted at a Council held at Westminster in 1338. Much of the money that was borrowed by Edward III to pay for his wars in France came from wool merchants; Fuller and Shepard made forced loans of £246 and £94 respectively.

Another Berkhamsted wool merchant, Adam Puff, had a worrying time in 1316. Off the Isle of Thanet, the Admiral of Calais captured a London ship destined for Antwerp with a cargo of wool worth £1,200. The largest individual owner was Puff, who had on board 21 serplers of wool valued at £210. He was compensated after protests, threats and the eventual seizure of French goods at Oxford and Southampton.

Flemish weavers were induced to settle in this country, passing on their knowledge to English craftsmen who soon equalled and then surpassed the skills of their tutors. In the reign of Richard II there was a subsidy of fourpence per broadcloth, and in 1387 thirteen Berkhamsted producers qualified for this subsidy, compared with 27 at St. Albans and five at Hertford.

Woodenware

The woollen industry waned, but through the centuries woodworkers have passed on their skills from one generation to another. It is a little unfortunate that two early craftsmen are known only because they were accused of stealing the Black Prince's timber; but they must have been specialists to bear such names as William the Turner and Richard the Shoveller.

By the mid-eighteenth century the local manufacture of wooden articles attracted the attention of William Ellis, a Little Gaddesden farmer and writer. He says:

The Berkhamsted and Cheshunt turners of hollow ware . . . make more consumption of this wood [alder] and beech than any other two towns in Great Britain, as is allowed by good judges: for with this wood they make dishes, bowls, and many other serviceable goods that are lighter and softer than the beech or elm, and will bear turning thinner than most others, so that to please curiosity, a dish of it has been turned inside out like a hat; and of this many of the matted and other chairs in London are made, as are pattens, clogs and heels of shoes, gates, hurdles and small rafters.

A century later, the 1851 census returns for Berkhamsted mention specialised trades such as those of the malt shovel maker, lath and hoop maker, plasterer's wood handle maker, rake maker, shaving box maker, chair-maker, coach-builder and boat-builder.

The first man to change ancient methods of production was Job East, who came from Chesham in 1840 to take over a small shovel-maker's and turner's business which had been started in the eighteenth century by a man named Austin. At first East used a saw-mill with horse-gearing attached, the only power to supplement manual labour. The business grew, and with ten men to help him East was soon the largest local employer in the trade.

Then came the Crimean War and contracts for lance poles, rammers for the artillery, shaving bowls and tent pegs and poles. Instead of ten men, East employed nearly a hundred. The business still flourishes at Gossoms End under the name of East and Son Ltd. Another firm of timber merchants was founded by William Key, a fencing contractor for the London and Birmingham Railway; the business continues under the name of J. Alsford Ltd.

In the 1880s, 200 men were employed at East's, Key's and several smaller timber yards; 50 worked for coach-builders, and 16 for a firm of boat-builders. A typical worker in one of the small timber yards was Joseph Tufnell, born in 1862, who worked from 6 a.m. to 6 p.m., except on Saturday, when he 'knocked off' at 4 p.m. He often had to help in the felling and carting of trees to the yard, where pit-sawing was the vogue. Fourpence an hour was considered a good wage for a skilled man. On piecework the payment was 4*d.* for a dozen whitewash brush handles, 4*s.* for a dozen malt shovels. A fast worker could make a malt shovel in half an hour.

By making brushbacks and handles by the thousand, the timber merchants were closely linked with the now defunct brushmaking industry, which in late Victorian times employed a hundred people, mainly girls and women.

Lace-Making and Straw Plaiting

In the eighteenth century, pillow lace making was a thriving cottage craft. Jingling gaily beaded bobbins, women worked on pillows to which were attached pricked parchment or cardboard patterns, glittering with pins to make a framework for the threads. The patterns were used over and over again.

That Berkhamsted was an important centre of the lace trade is suggested by the minting of a large quantity of halfpenny tokens bearing the words 'Pay at Leighton, Berkhamsted or London.' These tokens were issued by Chambers, Langston, Hall & Co., lace merchants and haberdashers, who organised production at Leighton Buzzard and also ran a shop and warehouse in London. One of the firm's partners lived in Berkhamsted. The tokens, bearing the date 1794, filled a useful need at a time when small change was scarce.

Lace-making was superseded in the nineteenth century by straw-plaiting. This too, was a cottage craft for women and girls whose 'chines' (machines) consisted of a straw splitter and a small mangle, called a mill. The splitter, made of wood, bone or iron, held cutters which resembled miniature wheels, with a varying number of razor-sharp spokes. In the middle of each wheel was a cone, on which each straw was centred before it was pushed through the cutter and sliced into the desired number of splints.

The sliced straws were pressed flat in the mangle, which was usually fastened to the kitchen door. Then the plaiting started, the workers customarily holding the straws in their mouths. Speed depended upon the skill and variety of plait required; the most popular local varieties were China Pearl, Rock Coburg and Moss Edge.

The finished plait was cut into lengths of 20 yards, known in the trade as scores. Practised workers could judge the exact length by winding the plait over their arms; others cut niches in the mantelpiece to serve as measuring aids.

In every town and village children were sent to straw-plaiting schools; it was rare for any other subject to be taught. At one time there were three plaiting schools in Bridge Street alone. In 1950 an elderly woman at Potten End told me that, as a small girl, she attended a plaiting school at Frithsden from 8 a.m. to 4 p.m., with a short break for dinner, usually consisting of bread and lard. After returning home for tea, she had to go to another plaiting school in Potten End. The children were sometimes taught in the dark, to accustom them to working without looking at the plait.

Once a week the finished product was sold to agents of Dunstable and Luton hat-makers. Weekly markets for straw-plait were held at Berkhamsted, Tring and Hemel Hempstead, and when the demand was exceptionally keen the buyers visited the workers' homes or met them on the way to market.

Changing fashions and foreign competition eventually killed a cottage craft which, in more profitable times, was said to have made the poor saucy and caused a dearth of indoor servants.

Lane's Prince Albert Apple

Another casualty was a nurseryman's business founded in 1777 by Henry Lane. At first he specialised in hedging plants and attended markets with bundles of samples under his arm. He started at the right time, for hedges, previously uncommon, became the vogue. The business expanded rapidly, and throughout the nineteenth century Lane was among the town's largest employers, with a nursery business known throughout the country and capable of exporting grapevines to France, Germany and other wine-growing countries.

The apple known as Lane's Prince Albert gave the business its greatest advertisement. The original tree was in the garden of a house called 'The Homestead' (250 High Street, demolished in 1958 and replaced by shops). Thomas Squire, who lived at 'The Homestead', often experimented with seeds and cuttings, and on July 26, 1841, he planted out a small apple tree after cheering Queen Victoria and the Prince Consort as they drove through the town. He named the tree 'Victoria and Albert', and in due course it bore excellent, unusual fruit. Mr. Lane not only exploited 'Britain's latest apple' but substituted his own name for Queen Victoria's.

Sheep Dip

More famous than the Berkhamsted-born apple are the products of a firm founded by William Cooper in 1843. A veterinary surgeon, he came to Berkhamsted with his few belongings in a black carpet bag. In the teeth of much prejudice, he won the confidence of local farmers, though for some years the rewards were meagre. For staying up all night with a sick horse, tending it and supplying medicines, he charged half-a-crown.

William Cooper sought a remedy for scab and other diseases of sheep. Experiments at his house near the police station led to the invention of Cooper's Sheep Dip, destined to become a famous product in every sheep-raising country. The firm has its headquarters at Berkhamsted and manufactures a wide range of agricultural and veterinary products.

Breweries

Malt-making, already mentioned as the principal local industry in Elizabethan times, continued for generations. There was enormous consumption of beer, much of it literally home-brewed, before tea and coffee found their way to the breakfast table. Among the many residents who had their own brewhouses was the master of the Bourne School. At Newhouse Farm, Castle Hill, Noah Newman provided free beer from the farm brewhouse for his sixteen labourers, whose combined wages came to £11 a week in 1850. No doubt it was the supplementary benefit which kept the men and boys happy.

Publicans had their own brewhouses until they found it more convenient to buy from another local brewer. It was the men who supplied beer to two, three, four or more public-houses who started the process which, via successive amalgamations, has created the giant brewery concerns of today. The former Swan Brewery in Chesham Road seems to have been one of the old-style brewhouses which originally supplied only the Swan Inn. Fosters, the last owners of the brewery, supplied the Swan, Brownlow Arms, Rose and Crown and two off-licences in Berkhamsted, as well as the Pheasant at Northchurch, the Eagle at Leighton Buzzard, the Eagle at Bierton, and an off-licence at Aylesbury. The business was taken over by Chesham Brewery in 1897. The name Foster is still visible on a former malthouse in Chapel Street, which has been a meeting place for boy scouts for as long as their grandparents can remember.

Until the Swan Brewery closed down in 1897, sixty men and boys were employed by local brewers. Locke and Smith, by far the larger firm, owned a brewery in Water Lane; it was taken over by Benskins of Watford and closed shortly before the 1914-18 war. Locke and Smith supplied nearly forty licensed houses: the Goat, Boat, Lamb, Bell, Boot, White Hart, Stag, Crooked Billet and George and Dragon in Berkhamsted and Northchurch, and the Plough at Potten End.

Watercress

Water, pure spring water, was required for the cultivation of watercress, an industry started in Victorian times. In 1883 the *Berkhamsted Times* congratulated Mr. Bedford on converting, at great cost and labour, 'dirty ditches and offensive marshes to pleasing watercourses in which grows a most healthy product. He has created a new industry which affords employment to many men.' Mr. Bedford sent two tons of watercress daily to northern towns; similar quantities from Bourne End and Chesham were also despatched from Berkhamsted railway station.

In more recent times several new industries have been introduced to Berkhamsted; large business concerns have also set up head offices in the town. More varied employment is available for Berkhamstedians than ever before, though with larger manufacturing and commercial centres within easy travelling distance many hundreds of local residents spend their working hours away from Berkhamsted.

The Local Press

A weekly newspaper started at Aylesbury as the *Buckinghamshire Herald* on July 18, 1792, was transferred to Berkhamsted after only eighteen issues and retitled the *Buckinghamshire, Bedfordshire and Hertfordshire Herald*. It was printed by W. McDowall and appeared weekly for about a year, the last issue being dated November 23, 1793. With the exception of the *Hartford Mercury*, started in 1772, the *Herald* was the only newspaper that was actually printed in Hertfordshire before 1825. It consisted of four small pages, each with five columns, and was edited by J. Webster. The price was $3\frac{1}{2}d$. For many years after the *Herald* was discontinued, or continued in another form elsewhere, W. McDowall's printing office produced books for Berkhamsted School. It is doubtful whether a copy of the newspaper still exists, but No. 7, Volume II, must have been available to the writer of an article which appeared in the *Berkhamsted Times* in 1892; besides quoting news items from the *Herald,* the article states that McDowall, the printer, also sold a sore throat ointment and toothache medicine.

The first newspaper with the name of Berkhamsted in the title, the *Chesham Recorder and Berkhampstead Advertiser*, was a short-lived venture started at Chesham in 1868. The *Berkhamsted Times,* printed in the town from 1875 until it was absorbed by the *West Herts and Watford Observer* in 1900, was edited for many years by Mr. George Loosley, publisher of the *Berkhamsted Directory*. Another Berkhamsted-born newspaper, the *West Herts Post,* first appeared in 1887; a few years later it was transferred to Watford, ceasing publication in 1970. Mr. F. J. King, who printed the *Post,* brought out the *Berkhamsted Express* in 1896; this had a very short life.

The *Berkhamsted Gazette* was started by Mr. Edgar Needham in 1904 as a 'daughter' of the *Hertfordshire, Hemel Hempstead Gazette,* founded in 1859. A very small newspaper, the *Berkhamsted Independent,* was started in 1921 and ran for four months.

The *Berkhamsted Review*, a church magazine with a large circulation, was started in 1872.

VIII
Market, Shops and Inns

BERKHAMSTED'S oldest institution is the street market. Evidence of its great antiquity is the changing of market day from Sunday to Monday in 1217, during the time of the building of St. Peter's Church beside the market place. In many parishes the clergy fulminated against trading on the Sabbath, but it is not known whether Berkhamsted traders were guilty of the not uncommon practice of setting up stalls in the churchyard.

There was great rivalry between market towns, and monopolies and concessions were eagerly sought. By royal charter, Berkhamsted men were excused payment of tolls wherever they went, but it could not have been easy to claim this exemption. In the Black Prince's time, the bailiff of Aylesbury demanded toll from Berkhamsted men, and in retaliation Aylesbury goods were distrained at Berkhamsted.

It was also decreed that no other market town was to be set up within eleven miles of Berkhamsted. At that distance, give or take a mile or so, are the ancient market towns of Dunstable, Aylesbury, High Wycombe and St. Albans. Privilege and prosperity did not always go hand in hand, for when the castle was abandoned the market declined, and Hemel Hempstead, ignoring Berkhamsted's territorial rights, started a market which captured most of the trade.

In the reign of Elizabeth I, the inhabitants hoped to improve the town's status as a trading centre by erecting a market house. A bold site at the top of Water Lane, intruding a little upon the highway, was chosen. The market house, with a loft for the storage of corn, stood on twenty oak posts, the lower part being open on all four sides. But trade continued to stagnate. Norden's survey of 1616 says the market was 'almost quite overthrown' and sales of corn were small compared with those in neighbouring towns.

Hopes were raised anew when James I's charter (1618) gave Berkhamsted the right to keep 'one markett on Thursday in every weeke, besides ye ancient markett kept on Munday.' In addition, there were to be two new fairs, 'one on Shrove Munday and ye other on Whitson Munday in every yeare, besides ye ancient faire on St. James's Day.' But the market still failed to attract more than a very small number of buyers and sellers. Smallpox epidemics were blamed for keeping customers away in the seventeenth century. Lipscomb in his *Journeys* described the market as 'shabby and decayed' in 1799.

The market house stood for over 250 years. Among the stout oak posts a few fortunate stallholders sheltered from rain if not from wind; other stalls spilled over the footpath and roadway. As the town's largest coaching inn stood almost opposite, traffic congestion probably caused high words between coachmen and carters.

Some residents considered the market house an unsightly obstruction. A carpenter tried to bring the structure to the ground by sawing through the posts, but stout oak filled with nails blunted the saw and he made a public fool of himself. At least he was spared the indignity of being placed in the stocks, which, to ensure maximum publicity for petty offenders, stood in front of the market house. A document of 1588 refers to the market house, 'where the pillorye now standeth.'

One night in August 1854, fire completely destroyed the market house. The burning question was whether the blaze was accidental or started deliberately. Tongues wagged knowingly, and one outspoken critic of the 'eyesore' was relieved to have a perfect alibi: business had detained him many miles from Berkhamsted on the night of the fire. In the 1930s I interviewed two nonagenarians, one of whom, William Fisher, was a member of the brigade which saved the fire from spreading to the Bell public-house a yard or two away;

The Market House and Five Bells Inn

the other, Mrs. C. Osborn, remembered Mrs. Dormer and Mr. Stone, who came over from Chesham to sell cakes, sweets and fruit under the old market house.

Two months after the fire, a public meeting was held at the King's Arms Inn to discuss the provision of a new market house, 'suitable to the increasing prosperity of the town.' William Hazell, a grocer, found a new site at a cost of £823, and public subscriptions were invited for an ambitious scheme, comprising a market house and chambers for the storage of corn, a town hall, a reading room for the Mechanics' Institute (founded locally in 1845), and magistrates' and committee rooms. The building cost £3,291, and most of the money was raised by the time the opening ceremony was performed in August 1860. The Sessions Hall was added in 1890. The whole property, administered by a committee elected annually by the ratepayers, was taken over by the Urban Council in 1971.

The building of a new market house did not revive Berkhamsted's ancient importance as a market town. But there was one annual event which brought crowds and chaos to the market place: the Michaelmas statute fair, known as the 'statty.' Stalls and sideshows lined both sides of the street, often bringing traffic to a standstill. Eventually the 'statty' died through lack of support. One other ancient fair continued until mid-Victorian times: this was the Whitsun fair granted by James I, which in later if not in early years was held on the Common and was apparently devoted to entertainment.

Loosley's Directory of 1882 mentions a cattle market on alternate Wednesdays, a market for straw-plait every Thursday, and a miscellaneous market on Saturday. By the turn of the century the straw-plait market had vanished, but the *Victoria History of Hertfordshire* still credited Berkhamsted with three market days: one for vegetables on Tuesday, another for meat and flowers on Saturday, and a cattle market on alternate Fridays, 'all so small as to be scarcely noticeable.'

The market rights, vested for many years in the owners of Ashridge, were acquired by the Town Hall Committee for a nominal sum a few years after the first World War, and transferred to the Urban Council in 1971. Market rights extend over the original footpath on both sides of the street from the Sayer almshouses to the parish church, but for many years the stalls have been confined to one side of the street, from Lower King's Road to Water Lane.

Shops

Little is known of the town's shops in early times. 'Le Shopperowe' is first mentioned in the Register of the Black Prince (November 3, 1357). Most of the early shops are better described as workshops, kept by craftsmen who made all, or nearly all, the goods they sold. Shopkeepers who did not produce anything at all themselves but bought and sold other people's goods were in a minority for many centuries.

From early times tradesmen were required to give customers a fair deal. Tasters of flesh, bread and beer were appointed annually; any man found guilty of selling food and drink of insufficient quantity or at too high a price was punished at the portmote court. Bakers, brewers, alehouse-keepers, mercers, drapers, grocers, chandlers, butchers, weavers, millers, glovers, etc., were required to 'appear with their weights and measures to have them tested by the standards.' For this purpose the Corporation of Berkhamsted kept a brass ell, a brass pint pot, a brass half peck and other measures.

It was unlawful to trade without having served an apprenticeship. In 1658 Henry Sears, shoemaker, and John Bilby and Stephen Stanley, bakers, were prosecuted, as was Charles Edge, a yeoman, who in 1663 evidently thought that he could make a better living by dyeing. At this period small change was scarce and several tradesmen issued tokens, usually for a halfpenny. John Seeling (1665), John Carvell (1667), William Babb (1667), and William Preston (1668) circulated tokens bearing their names.

In contrast to the scanty information available about shops and shopping in ancient times, there are many helpful sources in the various trade directories which first appeared in the latter half of the eighteenth century. The *Universal Directory* for 1792 seems to be the earliest to publish the names of local tradesmen: 98 in Berkhamsted, 57 in Northchurch. Some were farmers and others who would not have kept shops, but it seems that there were about 50 shopkeepers in Berkhamsted (population 1,350) and half-a-dozen in Northchurch (population 650).

Most of those early shops occupied the front parlours of cottages. Here and there a bow window helped the owners to display their wares, but the popular way of attracting customers, if the weather was fine, was to place the goods on trestles outside the shop.

Competition was keen, as is known by the presence of nine grocers in Berkhamsted and three in Northchurch when the 1792 directory was compiled. One grocer was also a cooper, another a gardener, another a spoonmaker, another a weaver. Yet another was a tallowchandler and draper as well as a grocer.

Not every bootmaker stuck to his last. Josiah Sale was also a tailor, capable of clothing his customers from head to boot. One of the four butchers was also a victualler, offering both meat and drink to his clients.

In 1792 Berkhamsted had one clockmaker, one ironmonger, one framework-knitter, several lace merchants and one peruke-maker. There was but one bookseller and stationer, but paper could be bought direct from John Barney Sumner, who made it at his home in Northchurch.

Two editions of *Pigot's Directory*, for the years 1824 and 1839, show how the town's shopping facilities grew apace during a period which included the building of the railway, when hundreds of extra workmen were here. The number of bakers increased from six to eight, bootmakers from eight to twelve, butchers from five to nine, tailors from five to seven, grocers from ten to 23. Berkhamsted also acquired a pawnbroker's shop.

At irregular intervals between 1882 and 1934, George Loosley and his son Albert published the *Berkhamsted Directory*. It is interesting to trace the rise and fall of certain trades and services. One by one the corn chandlers, hay and straw merchants, saddlers, farriers, coach-builders and wheelwrights—men whose livelihoods depended upon horses and horse-drawn traffic—went out of business. Servants' registry offices and brushmakers' and basketmakers' shops closed down. In 1890 Berkhamsted shoppers could call upon the services of ten tailors, eleven dressmakers, three laundresses, four watchmakers, seven coal merchants and twenty-four bootmakers. Although milk was delivered three times daily, one could buy further supplies of milk, cheese, cream and butter at several dairies or creameries, as the shops were called.

From early times most of the town's shops have been in the High Street; Lower King's Road, built in 1885, was without shops until the early years of this century. Previously there were many shops in Castle Street.

A new type of retailing was introduced by the Berkhamsted Co-operative Society in 1883; a modest start was made by asking 'mine host' of the Red Lion, on the Midland Bank site, to sell certain goods and provisions to members of the society. The co-operative movement grew quickly, occupying shops in several parts of the town, but all the business is now transacted in the High Street store, which was opened in 1933.

Inns and Public-houses

Unlike the shops, the taverns of the town diminish in number. In the 1890s the people of Berkhamsted and Northchurch could slake their thirsts at thirty different ports of call. By 1972 the population had more than doubled, but there were only seventeen inns and public-houses. Not since the Rising Sun heralded the dawn a century ago has a new public-house been licensed, though in the meantime several older establishments have been rebuilt.

If navvies had not created a disturbance at the Five Bells in the 1860s, thereby causing 'mine host' to lose his licence, the ancient building next door to the Civic Centre would probably still be devoted to beer instead of television sets. On the opposite side of the street stood the Bell, popularly called the 'One Bell' to distinguish it from the hostelry with five bells on the signboard. As already mentioned, the Bell narrowly escaped destruction by fire when the neighbouring market house was burnt down in 1854. The public-house survived until 1959 and was replaced by a shop.

Casualties have been high in Castle Street and Mill Street. The Castle and the Railway Tavern, facing the original railway station, and the Gardener's Arms at the corner of Chapel Street, were closed in 1966-8. The Boote still bears its name, but it became a private house soon after the first World War. Mill Street, having lost the Fish and the Edward VI, is now 'dry'.

In the High Street, the Queen's Arms closed its doors in 1968 after serving customers for more than 350 years. Perhaps it was never busier than in 1723, when 358 men and women called to sign the oath of allegiance to George I.

The White Hart, built in 1861, a year after its neighbour, the Town Hall, was closed in 1972. It is believed to have occupied the site of the Saracen's Head, which became the George in the reign of Henry VIII and then the Prince's Arms. This was among the properties given by John Incent for the endowment of Berkhamsted School in early Tudor times.

Earlier in this century the Red Lion was replaced by the Midland Bank and the Royal Oak by the Gas offices. Gossoms End lost its Stag, Northchurch its Anchor, Bell, Compasses and Pheasant, and Dudswell its Swan.

But all is not lost. At the east end of the town the Bull hides early 17th century work beneath brick and roughcast. The Black Horse is probably of 18th century origin. The Goat is a mid-19th century rebuilding of a straw-thatched pub that was a favourite haunt of drovers, who pounded their cattle in the three closes that name a nearby lane.

The Brownlow Arms, in Raven's Lane, is also a rebuilding of an early Victorian pub; its nearest rival, the Boat, started life as a farmhouse, and looks most attractive from the towpath. From the canal bridge it is only a short walk to the Rising Sun, with a front door which faces the towpath, not a street. The Crystal Palace, rebuilt in 1854 and much altered in 1867 and 1968, started life as a small beerhouse near the original railway station; at one time it was called the Engine Inn.

The George, among much eighteenth century work, contains fragments of a late sixteenth century timber-framed house. The Lamb looks old and charming, but little is known of its history. The Carpenter's Arms and the Rose and Crown have both been in business for about a century.

At Northchurch, the George and Dragon was a coaching inn; its yard was gay at the time of the village statute fair. Both the Crooked Billet and the Old Grey Mare, though modern buildings, have long ancestries.

Back to the heart of Berkhamsted for a quick glance at 'inn row', between Chesham Road and Prince Edward Street. The seventeenth century Swan is mentioned in many old documents, but no one has ever found the secret tunnel which is said to link the cellar with the parish church crypt. In the nineteenth century the Swan was kept by the Foster family, who brewed beer on land behind the inn (p. 73).

The Crown is a most interesting and attractive building, probably sixteenth century in origin but much modernised. For many years it was known as the Chaffcutters' Arms, but resumed its old name, the Crown, in 1852.

Next door to the Crown, the King's Arms bears the arms not of a king but of Queen Anne. Much of the town's business has been transacted within its early eighteenth century (and later) walls. Here, in 1833, a meeting of protest against the building of the railway was held, no doubt to the satisfaction of 'mine host', who, more than any of his rivals, benefited from the coaching trade.

Queen Victoria and the Prince Consort tarried awhile at the King's Arms for the horses to be changed. At an earlier date a French king, Louis XVIII, was a regular caller; during his long exile he found the King's Arms a happy as well as a convenient stopping place on his journeys between London and Aylesbury. The king's friendship with the innkeeper's daughter, Polly Page, is told on page 113.

Polly's father, John Page, kept the King's Arms for nearly fifty years and was high constable of Berkhamsted; for a short period he was also postmaster. John brewed his own beer, using furze from the Common for fuel, and had a farm in Billet Lane to supply fresh produce for his family and guests. He died in 1840 at the age of 92, a splendid advertisement for his home-grown food and drink.

IX
River, Road, Canal and Railway

THE RIVER, highway, canal and railway are so close together that cartographers must despair of showing four separate lines on small-scale maps. The first to be omitted is invariably the river which gives the Bulbourne valley its name.

Once a vigorous chalk stream, the Bulbourne created unhealthy marshland, causing an eighteenth century writer to say that Berkhamsted stretched along the south side of a swamp. There are still some pretty stretches of the river between its source at Dudswell and its union with the Gade at Two Waters, a distance of nearly seven miles, but the Bulbourne has lost most of its water to the canal, and watercress beds occupy some of the old marshland.

Besides providing 'fresh fishe' for the lord of the manor, the Bulbourne drove the wheels of two watermills, Upper Mill in Mill Street and Lower Mill in Bank Mill Lane. No doubt the mills, both mentioned in Domesday Book, were rebuilt several times during the the centuries when water and wind were the only sources of power that supplemented human and animal labour.

Until the early years of this century the Bulbourne continued, sometimes very fitfully, to drive the millstones. Corn for grinding arrived by the wagon-load and sometimes in small sacks and baskets brought by gleaners. When the Upper Mill was replaced by the Music School in 1926, a half-circular wall was built in Mill Street, bearing a Latin inscription which may be translated as follows:

> Here for a thousand years the old mills stood
> And gave us bread;
> Here now our School in rival motherhood
> Feeds minds instead.

The Highway

High Street is part of a Belgic track which became a Roman road and was known as Akeman Street in Saxon times. Though never so important as Watling Street, it has always been a well-used highway.

In Tudor times, when increasing use was made of wagon and coach, efforts were made to improve highways which had received little attention since the Roman occupation. Able-bodied men were required to work without payment six days a year on road repairs, but this duty was largely evaded and rates were levied for the upkeep of the roads.

It was the turnpike system which brought many highways into a fair state of repair. The first Turnpike Act was passed in 1663,

A SHORT HISTORY OF BERKHAMSTED

authorising the Justices of the Peace of Hertford, Cambridge and Huntingdon to levy tolls upon road users for the maintenance of highways, the tolls being collected at bars or turnpikes. The first tollbar was erected in Hertfordshire, at Wadesmill. Turnpike trusts were not numerous before 1750; then, in the next twenty years, the number was trebled.

In 1762 the Sparrows Herne Trust was formed with power to amend, widen, alter and keep in repair the road from the south end of Sparrows Herne, Bushey Heath, through the market towns of Watford, Berkhamsted and Tring, to the outskirts of Aylesbury, a distance of about 27 miles. The first meeting of the trustees took place at the King's Arms Inn in July 1762, and many subsequent meetings were held in Berkhamsted.

Among the original subscribers was Mary Essington, of Berkhamsted, who in 1763 gave to the parish, for the benefit of the poor, 'two bonds, certificates or securities for the sum of £210, advanced and lent by her on the credit of the tolls of the turnpike,' with interest at 5 per cent.

Men employed to improve the highway were paid 6s. a week. The trustees took advantage of statutory obligations and asked parochial surveyors of highways to supply lists of persons liable to work on the roads without payment. However, commutation (payment in lieu of labour) was allowed. Work was not to be demanded at harvest or haytime.

Four tollgates were erected, two outside Watford (where the inhabitants of Watford and Bushey were exempted from tolls when going to market), another at Newground, between Berkhamsted and Tring, and a fourth at Aston Clinton. Proposals to erect tollgates at the east and west ends of Berkhamsted were always defeated. It was not unknown for wagoners and others to drive into neighbouring fields to avoid payment of toll, and fences were erected to prevent anyone driving off the highway.

In 1823 the powers of the trust were enlarged. Much money had been borrowed and could not be repaid, and the tolls were increased. For a 'chariot, calash, chaise, hearse, etc.' the charge was 4½d. For cows the toll was 10d. a score, and for sheep 5d. a score.

The end of the Sparrows Herne Trust did not come until November 1, 1873, after most similar trusts had ceased to function. An iron post bearing the name of the trust still stands outside a shop at the top of Park Street; it adjoins an old stone at the boundary of the parishes of Berkhamsted and Northchurch and does not, as is sometimes thought, indicate that a tollbar formerly stood at this point.

The coaching days brought prosperity to many innkeepers. At the King's Arms, Nash relates in *Reminiscences of Berkhamsted*, horses with their riders were kept in readiness to obey the call at the shortest notice. The vehicles most in use were the yellow post-chaises drawn by two and sometimes four horses, according to the means or the importance of the travellers. The postillions were dressed in gay coloured jackets, white hats, booted and spurred, and he was the favourite rider who could force his horses over the stage of twelve miles in the shortest space of time. . . . To see a carriage and pair bespattered with dirt rattling through the town and suddenly pulling up in front of the hotel, was always sufficient to arrest the attention of a few loungers, and to give rise to a little harmless gossip. If the occupants of the carriage should happen to be a lady and gentleman of youthful appearance, their curiosity was more than usually aroused, and the onlookers would begin to speculate as to the probability of its being an elopement and their destination Gretna Green.

Travel by coach was slow. When John Yeoman visited relations at Berkhamsted in 1774, he left London at 7.30, had breakfast while the horses were changed at Stanmore, and arrived at Berkhamsted at 2 o'clock. According to the *Universal British Directory* of 1792, the fare from Berkhamsted to London by the Banbury and Birmingham coach was 8*s.* for an inside seat; by the Berkhamsted coach it was 7*s.* In 1810 the fare was 10*s.* for an inside seat, and 6*s.* for an outside seat. Poor people walked, or travelled with Thomas Bawthorn, the common carrier, whose wagons ran between Berkhamsted and London twice weekly. Nash refers to

those broad-wheeled wagons that were constantly passing through the town laden with merchandise and piled up to an enormous height and usually drawn by eight powerful horses. . . . If it was esteemed a privilege to walk by the side of the wagon, it must have been a still greater privilege, for a trifling consideration, to have been allowed to occupy a vacant space in the tail end of one of these vehicles. In those days it was very common to see the anxious traveller wending his way to some desired haven at the rate of two-and-a-half miles per hour. Sometimes whole families were to be seen travelling in this fashion with all their worldly possessions, migrating from one place to another.

The Canal

That the work of several men with several horses and wagons could be done by one canal boat drawn by one horse and attended by one man and a boy was proved by the third Duke of Bridgewater, of Ashridge (p. 91). It is pleasant to recall that in years gone by many a Sunday school treat started with a trip by horse-drawn canal boat from Castle Street to Newground, the children and teachers then continuing on foot or by wagonette to Moneybury Hill, above Aldbury, where the tall Bridgewater monument honours 'the father of inland navigation.'

The Grand Junction Canal Company was formed in 1793 to link the Thames with canals in the industrial Midlands. An army of 'navigators' (the canal labourers who added the word 'navvy' to our language) descended upon the district, living in special camps and offending staid townspeople by their drunken orgies.

As the work proceeded it was noted approvingly that the canal was draining away much of the stagnant overflow from the Bulbourne. The first hump-back bridges were built, and in Castle Street the road was raised by several feet, giving a row of half-timbered cottages, formerly level with the road, a curious sunken appearance. These cottages were demolished in 1964.

The Berkhamsted section was costly. In the few miles between Boxmoor and the Cow Roast, it was necessary to construct twenty of the fifty-five locks which were required to raise barges from the Thames to the Chiltern gap.

The Grand Junction Canal was opened from Brentford to Tring in 1798 and the entire route was completed in 1805. It was an immediate financial success, and shareholders were not the only beneficiaries. For the first time coal reached this district in large quantities at reasonable prices, though for many more years a large number of townspeople continued to burn wood or furze. Ambitious merchants built wharves, and a boat-building yard was established by John Hatton and continued by the Costin family between the busy Castle Street and Raven's Lane wharves. Until 'steamers' were introduced, all the boats were horse-drawn, and Albert Pocock, whose forge stood near the canal at Dudswell, shod as many as 100 boat horses a week. Canal workers had their favourite public-houses and shops and were especially fond of sheep's head and pluck for which Thomas Ashby, the Northchurch butcher, charged a shilling. The lock by New Road bridge was known to all boatmen as Sheep's Head Lock.

The Railway

In the 1830s a canal boat carried an unusual cargo: a steam locomotive. It was unloaded at Bourne End, assembled in a barn at Pix Farm, and used to haul trucks of earth from cuttings to build embankments for the canal's new rival, the railway.

Surveys for the line were started as early as 1825, and by 1830 two routes from London to the North were proposed: one via Oxford and Banbury, the other via Rugby and Coventry. George and Robert Stephenson, invited to report on the merits of the two routes, favoured the Coventry route, and subsequently Robert was appointed engineer to the London and Birmingham Railway Company, one of the predecessors of the famous London and North Western Railway Company. At one time there was a possibility that the line would run along the Gade, not the Bulbourne, valley. Fortunately Berkhamsted was not by-passed; it was among the first country towns in the world to have a station on a trunk railway.

Many were the landowners who objected to railways crossing their estates. Opposition was especially strong in Hertfordshire, and a resolution condemning the project was passed at a meeting held at the King's Arms, Berkhamsted. Perhaps the turnpike trustees, whose meetings were held at the same inn, were among the objectors. A similar protest meeting was held at Watford, where Lords Essex and Clarendon tried to keep iron horses off their Cassiobury and Grove Park estates. Among the obstinate landowners who likened railway pioneers to quacks and lunatics was Sir Astley Cooper, the surgeon, who is remembered in a happier connection as founder of Hemel Hempstead hospital. A line along the Gade valley would have run through his Gadebridge estate.

The owners of Ashridge were equally disturbed by the proposed route. Lord Brownlow, in the House of Lords on June 22, 1832, said that the case for the promotion of the London and Birmingham Railway Bill did not warrant 'the forcing of the proposed railway through the land and property of so great a proportion of dissentient landowners.' However, on May 6, 1833, the London and Birmingham Railway Act received the Royal assent.

In 1834, an army of workmen recruited by W. and L. Cubitt, contractors for the Berkhamsted section of the railway, assembled near the ruined barbican of the castle to receive their spades and wheelbarrows. It was known that the job would take two or three years, a very long time to wait for celebrations. After a short burst of activity, the men downed tools to enjoy unlimited beer for the rest of the day.

Cockney navvies, Irish labourers, bricklayers from the Midlands and miners from the North of England poured into Berkhamsted. Almost every cottage became a lodging house. At one period 700 men and boys were employed on the railway in this district alone; some of them married local girls, and their descendants are still living in Berkhamsted.

Public-houses were crowded, gang warfare sometimes broke out, and women were afraid to go out unescorted. Nash says:

> Some of the men were as brutal and ferocious as tigers, while there were others who were noble, manly fellows, and who, but for their drinking propensities, would have made their mark in the world in any pursuit of life. There were also a few among the foremen who, in addition to their superior intelligence, were remarkable for their sobriety and for their religious principles. It is to these men that Berkhamsted is indebted for the introduction of Wesleyanism into the town. . . .

Work could not have started at a more troublesome spot. It was necessary to build a high embankment over part of the outer moat of the castle, and powerful pumps were kept going night and day while workmen deposited 'a fabulous number of bricks into yawning caverns' to secure a firm foundation. It is said that there are more bricks below ground than those visible in the superstructure. A temporary bridge was thrown over the road to Whitehill, and earth from the Sunnyside cutting was taken by cart and wheelbarrow to complete the building of the embankment.

As soon as sufficient ground had been levelled to lay temporary rails, the 'Harvey Coombe,' the locomotive transported to Bourne End by canal boat, was puffing along with truckloads of soil from Northchurch tunnel and the Billet Lane cutting to build the long embankment between Bourne End and Boxmoor. The engine driver, Henry Weatherburn, was the son of one of George Stephenson's early workmates; he gave many residents a taste of railway travel before the line was officially opened.

Parish registers show that seven men, whose ages ranged from 18 to 26, were killed while helping to build the Berkhamsted section of the railway; in the parish of Northchurch there were at least four fatalities.

The first train ran from London to Boxmoor in July, 1837, and the line was opened as far as Tring on October 16 of the same year. Making an experimental trip in six carriages, directors and friends passed through Berkhamsted 59 minutes after leaving the terminus at Primrose Hill. The original railway station, almost opposite Castle Street, was praised for its 'Elizabethan style of architecture, which forms an agreeable relief to those of other stations, the whole of which are mere plain brick or stone erections.'

In 1838, three up and three down trains stopped at Berkhamsted on weekdays. First class passengers paid 8*s.* for the single journey from Berkhamsted to London, travelling in covered, upholstered carriages which were probably as rickety as the stage-coaches they resembled. Second class passengers paid 6*s.* 6*d.* to ride in coaches that were open at the sides.

To the two original tracks a third was added in 1857-9, and by that time travel was cheaper: 5*s.* first class, 3*s.* 6*d.* second class, 2*s.* 4*d.* third class. It was then possible to leave Euston at 4.15 and reach Berkhamsted by 5.8; this was our first 'under the hour' train.

In 1875, when the fourth track was added, a new station was built with extensive sidings to replace the old goods yard between the original station and Gravel Path. In 1887 the fastest train of the day left Berkhamsted at 8.54 a.m. and with one stop at Willesden reached Euston at 9.35; this speed was not greatly improved upon until the line was electrified in 1966.

Berkhamsted station was used by a large number of Chesham residents, who had to wait for a station of their own until Britain's last trunk railway, the Great Central, was built. In 1887 the cost of carrying goods between Berkhamsted station and Chesham was estimated at £10,000 a year. Complaints were made that Berkhamsted roads were being worn out by the Chesham traffic, and donations towards the cost of making Lower King's Road, built ten years after the new station was opened, were solicited from Buckinghamshire neighbours.

On several occasions the London and North Western Railway Company made vague promises to build a branch line to Chesham. No action was taken, but in 1887 the Chesham, Boxmoor and Hemel Hempstead Steam Tramway Company was promoted with the intention of laying rails along the main road from Marlowes, Hemel Hempstead, to Bourne End, and then along the valley of the Bourne Gutter to Ashley Green and Chesham.

The tramway enthusiasts of Berkhamsted, who expected the line to run from our railway station to Chesham via Kings Road, were so incensed by the proposed route that S. Sellon, the tramway engineer, promised to do all in his power to provide a branch line from Bourne End to Northchurch, with a spur from the Berkhamsted crossroads to the railway station. Meetings supporting or opposing the steam tramway were held in several parishes, and many were the objections that the roads were too narrow for trams and that the locomotives would frighten horses. The promoters were no less frightened by the heavy cost of an undertaking which was quickly and quietly forgotten.

Interest in an iron link between Berkhamsted and Chesham was revived when it was proposed that the Great Central's branch line from Chalfont Road to Chesham should be continued to Berkhamsted. Again, no action was taken.

Buses, Cars and Cycles

Belated efforts were made by the London and North Western Railway Company to retain some of the Chesham traffic. In 1899 'the newest form of locomotion, the motor-car,' was introduced to convey passengers between Berkhamsted and Chesham. This must have been one of the first public services of its kind in the country, and though short-lived—the motor-car was soon replaced by a horse-drawn vehicle—the railway company's experiment preceded by over twenty years the first local motor-bus service.

Above: The 'Harvey Coombe' has just passed under Gravel Path bridge, 1837

Below: View from Gravel Path bridge, *c.* 1870

Horse-drawn boat on the canal, 'iron horse' on the railway, c. 1840

The original railway station, opened in October 1837

Back Lane, showing, right, the One Bell public house and, extreme right, a part of the old Market House.

In Victorian times, Mr. H. Lane, of the King's Arms Hotel, started a 'town omnibus' service; every train was met and passengers were conveyed to any part of the town for sixpence, or to Northchurch for a shilling. Drawn by one horse, the bus had six inside seats and ample space on the roof for baggage.

The horse troughs and most of the horse ponds of Victorian days have vanished, but old residents have memories of a 'horsy' town with hundreds of carriages, carts and wagons. Jobmasters, saddlers, blacksmiths and hay and corn merchants were among the town's most prosperous tradesmen.

Cycling was popular, and a Berkhamsted man became famous for his travels with a 'penny farthing.' Thomas Stevens, born in Castle Street on Christmas Eve, 1854, was educated at the Bourne School and emigrated to the United States when he was about sixteen years old. In 1883 he bought a bicycle and pedalled and pushed it all the way from San Francisco to Boston in 104 days. This was the prelude to a world tour which lasted three years and included a visit to relations in Berkhamsted and a lecture at the Town Hall. Thomas Stevens described his adventures in several books. He returned to England in 1895 and died in London in 1935.

Towards the end of the nineteenth century, cyclists, horses and horse-drawn vehicles no longer had the roads to themselves. It is believed that the first Berkhamsted car owner was a shopkeeper, J. W. Wood, whose second-hand Benz was capable of tackling the steepest Chiltern hills. But on one occasion it came to grief on a level stretch of the highway near Broadway, and one carthorse was required to tow $4\frac{1}{2}$ horse-power to Berkhamsted's first garage, a greenhouse. Mr. Wood's son kept up the family pioneering spirit by riding the town's first motor-cycle, a Kerry.

For many years the most familiar make of motor-cycle in Berkhamsted was the Southey. In 1904 or thereabouts the local firm of C. E. Southey & Co. started building motor-cycles, and over 900 were sold before the business closed down between the two World Wars.

The first local motor omnibus service was started by an Aylesbury firm in 1920. Such was the novelty of the small bus which ran between Aylesbury and Berkhamsted that A. H. Sprigge, a men's outfitter at the corner of Prince Edward Street, advertised that his shop was 'where the bus turns round'. In 1921 the London and General Omnibus Company extended the Bushey-Boxmoor service to Berkhamsted, and in quick succession several other services were started by the National Omnibus and Transport Company, which agreed to operate the London company's services in Hertfordshire.

X
Ashridge

ASHRIDGE HOUSE, now the Ashridge Management College, stands on the site of a monastery that was always known as a 'house and college' in documents of the period. It owes its origin to a Berkhamsted man, Edmund Earl of Cornwall (p. 22), who, during a visit to Saxony, acquired a box which was said to contain some of Christ's blood. After presenting a portion of the holy relic to Hailes Abbey, he founded Ashridge in honour of the remainder, requiring the brethren to guard the relic and pray for the soul of his father 'until the world's end.' Unlike Hailes, however, there is no evidence that Ashridge became a great place of pilgrimage.

Building started in the mid-1270s, and Edmund is believed to have spent more time in his new house than at Berkhamsted Castle. Edward I stayed at Ashridge for several weeks in 1290, and in the following January held a parliament there. The Black Prince (p. 22) was so fond of Ashridge that he was regarded (and regarded himself) as its founder or re-founder; the last of his many gifts to the brethren was 'our great table of gold and silver . . . to the High Altar of our House of Asherugge, which is our foundation'.

The first rector, Richard of Watford, was installed with twenty brethren, of whom thirteen were priests according to the charter. They wore long grey tunics and ankle-length grey cloaks. Among their aims was the advancement of learning, and one of the brethren wrote 'A Lytell Treatise in Englyshe called the Extirpacion of Ignorancy'. Another work was entitled 'A Lytell Boke contayning certain gostly medycynes agens the comen plage of pestilence'.

Known as the Bonhommes (good men), the monks are mentioned by John Skelton, Henry VIII's poet laureate:

> Of the bone homs at Ashridge beside Barcanstede,
> That goodly place to Skelton most kynde,
> Where the sange royall is, Christis blood so rede,
> Whereupon he metrified after his mynde,
> A pleasanter place than Ashridge is harde were to finde . . .

Henry VIII found it a pleasant place, too, when he hunted in the park and visited his 'gentleman priest,' Thomas Waterhouse, in 1530. A servant was paid 7*s*. 6*d*. for 'bringing of a bucke to the King at Ashridge,' and 'Edmond the foteman' received 3*s*. 8*d*. 'for so muche by him gyven in reward at Assherige to one that made the dogges to draw water.' The dogs (replaced many years later by donkeys) were used to raise water from the very deep well.

Five years after the royal visit, the bell that had summoned the brethren to prayer for two and a half centuries sounded, in effect, the death knell of the monastery. It was suppressed by Henry VIII and the 'holy blood' was exposed as a fake. Thomas Waterhouse, the last rector, and some of the brethren remained in the district; Daniel Axtell, the regicide (p. 102), was descended from John Axtell, one of the Bonhommes.

Ashridge was not left to fall into ruin. For a short time it became one of the homes of Henry VIII's three children, Edward, Mary and Elizabeth.

Elizabeth retired to the house on the coronation of Mary, and spent many hours embroidering 'some of ye childe bed things' for the infant that was never born to the sister she had no cause to love. Mary, suspecting Elizabeth of being implicated in the Wyatt rebellion, ordered her arrest in 1553, and despatched commissioners to take her to the Tower of London. She was said to be too ill to travel, and by collapsing three times in the courtyard of Ashridge proved that she was either very ill or over-acting. No case could be proved against Elizabeth; a few years later she became Queen of England. In 1556, she leased Ashridge to Richard Coombe, of Hemel Hempstead, at an annual rent of £6 0s. 10d.

In 1604, Ashridge passed to Thomas Egerton, Elizabeth's Lord Keeper of the Seal and James I's Lord Chancellor. He restored and added to the monastic buildings; an estimate for furniture alone ran to twelve folios. His son and successor was created the first Earl of Bridgewater, and his influential and scholarly descendants held Ashridge for two centuries.

It was the least scholarly member who amassed the great wealth which, after his death, paid for the rebuilding of the ancestral home. Francis Egerton, born in 1736, was only twelve years old when he succeeded his brother and became the third Duke of Bridgewater. (His father, the fourth earl, married a daughter of the great Duke of Marlborough and was created the first Duke of Bridgewater in 1720.)

Jilted by a young, widowed duchess in 1759, Francis sought solace in the building of canals. He moved to Lancashire and became obsessed with a scheme that was primarily intended to reduce the cost of transporting coal from his mines at Worsley to Manchester. This canal was a very costly undertaking; the duke was often hard pressed to meet his bills, and his famous London home, Bridgewater House, was boarded up. Ashridge was neglected; rain poured through the roofs, canvasses in the picture gallery sagged from rotten frames, and mural paintings in the cloisters were ruined.

The duke's money, foresight and energy, and his faith in the engineering genius of James Brindley, eventually brought rich rewards.

He amassed the 'Bridgewater millions' and gained the title of 'father of inland navigation.' But to many of his contemporaries he was a gruff, eccentric bore, lacking a sense of humour and having little to talk about except his canal. His treatment of Brindley was scandalous, though some of his workers found him a fair, enlightened employer. His fondness for old, outmoded clothes, despite an income of over £110,000 a year, caused much comment; so did his dislike of women. But for all his odd ways, the duke was not so eccentric as his grand-nephew, the eighth earl, who lived in Paris and dined with his dogs dressed as human beings and waited upon by powdered flunkeys.

On returning to Ashridge, the duke stayed in the lodge, which was still in fair condition, and planned a great castle to replace the house he had left to go to rack and ruin. But he died in 1803, 'memorable among those who were honoured in their generation and were the glory of their times,' to quote his epitaph in Little Gaddesden Church. A more familiar monument, the tall column above Moneybury Hill, is a landmark for miles around.

Over half of the Bridgewater fortune was inherited by the bachelor duke's cousin, Lieut.-General John William Egerton, seventh Earl of Bridgewater. Rebuilding Ashridge on a grandiose scale at a cost of £300,000, he felt that he was discharging a sacred trust; his late cousin wanted a vast castle, and James and Jeffry Wyatt, the architects, provided an extravaganza. It was a preposterously large mansion for a childless, ageing couple, and slighting remarks were made about its ostentatious owner.

The destruction of the old house and the building of the new provided work for an army of masons and carpenters. The foundation stone was laid by Charlotte, Countess of Bridgewater, on October 25, 1808, and the house was inhabited in the autumn of 1814. The great drawing room, 50 feet long, was hung with crimson damask; the dining room and anterooms were sumptuously furnished. Yet these apartments, for all their magnificence, were dwarfed by the staircase hall, its walls rearing to a richly-ornamented ceiling and an interior wind-dial 95 feet above the floor. To this extravagant hall were added statues by Richard Westmacott of bygone Ashridge personages, including Edmund of Cornwall and the Black Prince. For the beautiful little chapel, rich sixteenth century stained glass was brought from Germany. It is now at the Victoria and Albert Museum.

For all his riches, the seventh Earl of Bridgewater could be as parsimonious as the 'canal duke,' but no one could accuse him of belonging to the idle rich. He was interested in new farming methods and kept a close eye on his vast estate. He provided new roads (in-

A SHORT HISTORY OF BERKHAMSTED

cluding the one from Northchurch to Ringshall) and started the good work of giving the labouring poor better houses. He was also the first owner of Ashridge to take a really close interest in local affairs and local people. Little escaped his notice, as we know from the diaries kept by his bailiff, William Buckingham. These diaries are now at the County Record Office, Hertford.

While Buckingham recorded everyday happenings, Archdeacon Todd wrote *The History of the College of Ashridge*. Like everything else associated with Ashridge at that period, it was a magnificent tome, full of fine plates. It appeared in 1823, the year of the seventh Earl's death; his widow remained at Ashridge and was a generous subscriber to good causes, especially schools. She died in 1849.

The seventh earl left an involved will which provided for his millions to go to whichever of several distant relatives should attain the dignity of a dukedom or marquisate. This provision was set aside by the courts and the estate eventually passed to the second Earl Brownlow (p. 95). Having extended the Ashridge estate by purchasing the manor of Berkhamsted from the Duchy of Cornwall, the Brownlows continued the work of building roads and schools. Many houses were built for estate workers, and Little Gaddesden, described as a model village of the period, was provided with piped water seven years before Berkhamsted.

Adelbert, third Earl Brownlow, started his long 'reign' at Ashridge in 1867, a year before his marriage to Lady Adelaide Talbot, youngest daughter of the Earl of Shrewsbury. They were familiar and popular figures in Berkhamsted and had their own private entrance to the railway station, where they met many of the famous people who were entertained at Ashridge. When the Shah of Persia arrived at Berkhamsted by special train in 1889, grandstands were erected outside the station and men of the Hertfordshire Yeomanry, in scarlet coats and steel, plumed helmets, escorted the royal party to Ashridge.

Following the death of the third Earl Brownlow in 1921, trustees were directed to sell Ashridge to meet death duties. The National Trust acquired 3,500 acres of the park, and in 1928 Mr. Urban Broughton, with Mr. (afterwards Lord) Davidson, bought the house with about 235 acres to establish a residential college affiliated to the Conservative Party. It was known as the Bonar Law Memorial College in memory of Broughton's great friend, who was prime minister from 1922–3. From 1939–46 Ashridge was an emergency hospital. Reopened as a college in 1947, it was shorn of party affiliations in 1954, and became a completely independent college in 1959, devoted to education for management.

XI
The Common and the Park

BERKHAMSTED COMMON is a large and beautiful remnant of the waste land of the manor. Many hundreds of acres of gorse, fern and woodland extend for nearly four miles from Potten End to within a short distance of Northchurch and Dudswell.

For centuries the Common was prized for the practical use that could be made of it. All common rights derived from a grant by the lord of the manor, whose tenants grazed cattle and sheep, and especially pigs in early times, on the waste. Flocks of sheep were still seen on the Common in the early years of this century, but by that time few people still exercised rights to take gorse for fuel and fern for litter. Sand and gravel were also taken from the Common

Unlike the present generation, our forebears had little if any interest in the preservation of the Common as an area of natural beauty. Thus, when the Duchy of Cornwall, in 1618, cast covetous eyes on the Common and enclosed 300 acres to 'improve' the land (and incidentally increase the rent roll) many people favoured the conversion of waste into agricultural land. It was a time of great land-hunger. The people who resented enclosure were commoners who exercised grazing and other rights. The Northchurch tenants were especially antagonistic, for they made greater use of the 300 acres than their Berkhamsted neighbours. What became known as the Coldharbour Enclosure was the start of a long feud between village and town.

The 300 acres taken out of the Common were added to Berkhamsted Park, over 1,000 acres of which were disparked (released for cultivation) in 1627. This event probably had a great effect on the economic life of the town. Many men were at last able to rent land, either to start their own farms and smallholdings or to add to the acres they already farmed. There was a great deal of land trading, and it seems that many more new acres were made available here than in many other parishes.

In 1639 the Crown was even more desperately in need of revenue and the Duchy of Cornwall proposed the enclosure of a large portion of the Common. As before, it seems that the Berkhamsted commoners were acquiescent. But the Northchurch tenants, who had grudgingly accepted defeat in 1618 on the understanding that there would be no more 'improvements,' were now in a rebellious mood.

William Edlyn, of Norcott Hill, believed in straight talking. For making speeches against the Duchy's proposal he was taken into custody. A short spell of imprisonment did not dampen the spirit of this village Hampden; words were followed by daring action as soon as the enclosure was made. In a night raid, the fences, hedges and rails were smashed down by a force of about 100 men, including a dozen soldiers who were billeted at Hemel Hempstead. Shortly afterwards, William Edlyn and other Northchurch ringleaders were arrested. They petitioned the Council of the Duchy to be placed on trial, to fight out the whole question of the legality of the enclosure, and were released: William Edlyn thereupon petitioned the House of Commons against 'grand and arbitrary oppression.'

The commissioners, instead of obeying the House of Commons' summons to produce witnesses and records, petitioned the House of Lords, stressing the 'violence' that had been used by the Northchurch tenants. William Edlyn, his son John, and Francis Fenn were arrested and brought before the Lords. Though satisfied that the men were delinquents, their lordships were pleased to 'remitt their offence,' with a caution that if they or others offended again they would be severely punished. They did, in fact, figure in another fence-smashing episode when the rector of Berkhamsted, Thomas Newman, tried to enclose twenty acres. Thanks largely to Edlyn, however, the Common remained unenclosed until 1866, when the owner of Ashridge fenced in an area very similar to the enclosure of 1640.

The Ashridge connection with Berkhamsted Common started in 1761, when the manor of Berkhamsted was leased by the Duchy of Cornwall to the Duke of Bridgewater. From the Bridgewaters Ashridge passed to the Brownlows, and in 1860 the trustees of the second Lord Brownlow, then 18 years old, learnt that the Prince Consort, guardian of the Duchy estates, was prepared to consider the sale of the manor of Berkhamsted. Agreement was eventually reached whereby the Brownlow trustees bought the manor for £144,546, of which £43,682 was for 1,332 acres of waste or common land, roughly £33 an acre.

By April 1865, Lord Brownlow's advisers felt that he had acquired sufficient interest to enclose Berkhamsted Common under the General Enclosure Act, and his agent, William Paxton, informed the Berkhamsted vestry that he was willing to give the town a central recreation ground 'as a just and liberal compensation in lieu of the existing trivial outstanding claims on the common.'

The recreation ground would have extended all the way from Mill Street to Billet Lane, between the Bulbourne and the railway, plus a few acres on the south side of the river at Gossoms End. Ten of the total of 43 acres were scheduled for garden allotments.

Many of the townspeople considered this a bargain, preferring a central recreation ground to the hilltop heathland a mile away. No fewer than 413 people signed away their rights, but a few withheld their signatures. Among them was Mr. Augustus Smith, a most uncommon commoner, who owned Ashlyns Hall and continued to take great interest in the town long after he had acquired the Isles of Scilly, of which he was known as the king or lord. His links with the west country were reinforced when he was elected M.P. for Truro, and in the House of Commons he annually asserted the rights of the public against the claims of the Crown and the Duchy of Cornwall to the ownership of the foreshore of the sea coasts. He had the qualities of courage and persistence which marked him out as the man best suited to fight the cause of the Berkhamsted commoners.

Matters came to a head early in 1866, when Lord Brownlow proceeded with the enclosure. An order for tons of fencing was placed with James Wood, a Berkhamsted ironfounder, whose workmen dug 2,640 holes, each three feet deep, for the uprights before proceeding with the erection of two miles of iron railings. A third (the central portion) of Berkhamsted Common was enclosed, preventing traffic from passing along ancient tracks from east to west, and excluding people who had pastured sheep or exercised other common rights.

At the House of Commons, one of the founders of the Commons, Open Spaces and Footpaths Preservation Society, Mr. George John Shaw-Lefevre (afterwards Lord Eversley) discussed the enclosure with Mr. Augustus Smith. As Lord Eversley says in *Commons, Forests and Footpaths* (1910), 'it was decided to resort to the old practice of abating the enclosure by the forcible removal of all the fences, in a manner that would be a demonstration, and an assertion of right, not less conspicuous than their erection.'

The action taken was prompt and sensational. A contractor recruited a private army, 120 strong, at Southwark for what he described as 'a night job at Tring,' and a special train was chartered to leave Euston station at midnight.

But the secret mission almost foundered when the train arrived at Tring at 1.30 a.m. on March 7, 1866. The men were without a leader. The contractor had sub-let his contract to another man, and at a public-house near Euston station the two drank themselves into a state that deprived them of the ability to direct even their own movements.

The situation was saved by a lawyer's clerk, who had been sent to watch the proceedings at a distance by Mr. P. H. Lawrence, solicitor to the newly founded Commons, Open Spaces and Footpaths

Augustus Smith

Lord Brownlow (Chapter XI) contributed £500 towards the cost of a new Town Hall

Preservation Society. G. H. Whybrow, whose *History of Berkhamsted Common* (1934) is now out of print, believes that the clerk who rallied the ranks and took command of the men as they marched two by two to Berkhamsted Common was named George Micklewright.

Hammers and chisels were used to loosen the substantial joints of the railings, then the uprights were uprooted and the metal bars were wrapped around them. Moonlight helped the night raiders and they completed the destruction of the fences in about four hours. It seems that no one other than the workmen heard the bangs and clatter.

At 7 a.m., an hour after the destruction was completed, William Paxton rode up to see the twisted ironwork. It could not have been a pleasant sight for the brother of Sir Joseph Paxton, designer of the iron-and-glass extravaganza in London known as the Crystal Palace.

William Paxton made an energetic protest. So did William Hazell, a Berkhamsted grocer, who was regarded as one of Lord Brownlow's chief yes-men. According to a poem which appeared in *Punch* shortly after the event, Hazell had to distribute beer money to escape a ducking in the canal when the navvies descended on Berkhamsted to celebrate a hard night's work.

A contemporary newspaper report says that 'in carriages, gigs, dog-carts and on foot, gentry, shopkeepers, husbandmen, women and children at once tested the quality of what they saw by strolling over and squatting on the common and taking away morsels of gorse to prove, as they said, the place was their own again.'

It was also necessary to take away the damaged railings, which had cost over £1,000. Mr. Wood was again called in, this time to estimate for the collection and repair of the ironwork. The price quoted, £186 14s. 2½d., suggests very careful estimating.

Legal proceedings were taken against Augustus Smith by Lord Brownlow, who later expressed a desire to settle the matter in an amicable manner and avoid a court of law; but Augustus Smith preferred 'the long prospect of litigation ... to secure the result intended.'

The action for trespass was never heard, for Lord Brownlow died in February 1867, just a year after the fences were erected. In the meantime Mr. Smith commenced a counter action, which dragged on for three years until judgment was given in his favour by Lord Romilly, Master of the Rolls. A right of common of pasture for all sorts of cattle, levant and couchant, was declared to exist, as was a right to cut furze, gorse, fern and underwood for fodder and litter for commonable cattle, but not a right of estovers, haybote and woodbote (referring to the cutting of timber for house repair, fuel, repairing hedges, fences, ploughs, rakes, etc.); the judge also negated what throughout the case was described as 'the right of recreation' on the Common.

However, the people of Berkhamsted continued to roam over the Common. The cordial relationship that normally existed between the Brownlows and the townsfolk was not seriously ruffled. The lord who enclosed the common was a quiet young man who had inherited the Bridgewater millions but could not buy the one good thing he lacked, a sound constitution. His mother, Lady Marion Alford, was undoubtedly the power behind the Ashridge throne, and when references are made to the ill advice Lord Brownlow received on the common enclosure, Lady Marion is apt to be singled out as the ill-adviser-in chief. But both mother and son deserve to be remembered for their good works, not for the arrogant lapse of 1866. They made new roads across the Common, and their purchase of the Duchy estate probably saved Berkhamsted Park from Victorian speculators. The second Earl Brownlow was succeeded by his brother Adelbert; he died in 1921 and the Ashridge estate was then sold to meet death duties.

The eastern portion of the Common was bought privately by Mr. Edwin Williams and presented by him to Berkhamsted Golf Club; trustees were appointed for the future administration of this area. The club lodged with the Ministry of Agriculture and Fisheries a deed of declaration giving people the right of air and exercise.

Other large portions of the Ashridge estate, including the western portion of Berkhamsted Common, were bought by public-spirited people, most of whom were local residents, to save as much open country as possible for the enjoyment of all. Started in 1925, the National Trust's Ashridge Estate now covers about six square miles in Hertfordshire and Buckinghamshire and includes five commons.

And so, thanks to William Edlyn, Augustus Smith and thousands of donors of our own times, we share with 67 different species of birds and 20 species of mammal the delights of a vast tract of outstanding natural beauty and historic interest.

The Greens

On the south side of the town, Brickhill Green, Sandpit Green and Long Green are linked by an ancient track which runs from Shootersway to Sugar Lane, Bourne End. Another little green adjoins Shootersway, between the top of Durrants Lane and Bell Lane; now only a narrow roadside waste, it is mentioned in old documents. In the seventeenth century a pest house for Northchurch was erected on the waste.

'One wast plott or moore lying by the river,' mentioned in a survey of 1616, survives as a small recreation ground known as the Moor. Another recreation ground—not ancient common land—is of great interest; Butts Meadow would have been built upon but for the intervention of Mrs. Lionel Lucas, of Kingshill, who purchased the land in 1886 and gave it to the town. The site of the butts and the place where the archers stood to shoot could be traced until 1932, when, to provide work at a time of much unemployment, the meadow was levelled. Velvet Lawn, a recreation ground at the top of Swing Gate Lane, was given to the town by the Foundling Hospital in compensation for the loss of a right of way from Three Close Lane to Ashlyns.

The Park

For the good management of Berkhamsted Park an officer known as the parker was appointed regularly. In 1302, 'William called Hereford of Berchampstede' was given custody of 'the wood, park and warren,' receiving $5\frac{1}{2}d.$ a day and all windfallen timber. He was responsible for preserving the game and was authorised to buy hay specially to feed the deer in winter.

In the Black Prince's time the parker and other officers were men who had served with him in the French wars. Robert le Parker, in 1346, held office 'for good service to the King and the Prince,' and was in charge of both the Park and the Common, receiving $2d.$ a day and 'a robe of the livery of the Prince's craftsmen.' In 1347 he was ordered to take 'a buck of grease' (a fat buck) to the Abbot of St. Albans. In 1335, when the Park was completely fenced in, the Black Prince cut down and sold beeches on the Common to buy oak palings for the Park.

The reduction of the Park from 1,132 to 375 acres in 1627, the disparked land being used for farming, was mentioned earlier in this chapter.

A short-lived development at the end of the nineteenth century was a nine-hole golf course across the Park, made for players who found the original nine-hole course on the Common a little too remote. A hut for club members stood in the castle grounds.

'Kitchener's Army,' followed by the Inns of Court Officers' Training Corps, camped and trained in the Park and erected a number of large huts, which were removed when the first World War ended. The name 'Kitchener's Field' is still used.

XII
In Stuart Times

BERKHAMSTED lost enthusiasm for the monarchy in the second quarter of the seventeenth century. Most of the townfolk, like most of the people of Hertfordshire, sided with Parliament. In the reign of James I, however, this was still a royal, loyal town, proud to receive honour and bounty from the King, who granted Berkhamsted a new charter and gave £100 to the poor of the parish. Not since the days of the Black Prince had a Prince of Wales and Duke of Cornwall been welcomed so warmly as Charles (afterwards Charles I) who, as a youth of 16, came to Berkhamsted in 1616. Twenty horsemen met him at Brickhill Green corner and escorted him down Chesham Road and Castle Street, where he stopped to hear a speech of welcome in Latin by 'one of the Schollers of the free schole.' The prince then proceeded to Berkhamsted Place, newly leased to his former tutor Thomas Murray. In the afternoon, Charles hunted in the park, killed a fat buck, and gave it to his attendants.

On a later occasion Prince Charles listened sympathetically to complaints that Berkhamsted men, exempted by ancient royal charter from attendance at assizes and sessions, were nevertheless summoned for jury service. A letter preserved in the church chest states that Charles ordered the High Sheriff to 'forebeare to somon or to retourne anie of the said Tennants or Inhabitants for the services aforesaid.' The prince's interest in the town is further shown by his gift of £100 in 1620 to provide employment for the poor; on his accession to the throne six years later he gave another £100 to the poor, this time to supply wood for firing.

There was no readiness to give anything back when Charles demanded Ship Money. Payment of the £25 levy on Berkhamsted was 'longe behynde' in 1638. The king and queen passed through Berkhamsted in 1636, and in contrast to the town's ebullient welcome to Charles twenty years earlier, it seems that the royal visit was shunned. The Corporation record book acknowledged 'the blame that was layd upon us by neglecting our formal attendance and presents to the kinge and queene.'

It was an age of mounting political and religious fervour. How the mood of certain commoners changed from sullen acquiescence to open defiance is shown in Chapter XI. In 1618, men grumbled bitterly but did not take the law into their own hands when part of Berkhamsted Common was enclosed. Some twenty years later, however, the fences of another enclosure were smashed down by commoners who were determined to fight for their rights, whatever the consequences.

Berkhamsted had its own little civil war three years before the great Civil War broke out.

In June 1643, the countryside rang with stories that Ashridge House had been plundered. The Earl of Bridgewater, nominally a Parliamentarian, reported to the House of Lords that Captain Washington, Captain Kemsey and Captain Burr, with their soldiers, entered his park and house at Ashridge. They 'detained his servants prisoners,' beat down ceilings, broke open and hewed down doors, searched all the Earl's evidences, rooms, studies and closets, took away plate, arms, etc., destroyed all his deer, and made off with 44 horses.

A month later, water pipes at Berkhamsted Place were broken and carried away to spite the Royalist tenants 'in these troublesome tymes.'

Alfred Kingston, in *Hertfordshire During the Civil War,* says that Berkhamsted, 'situated on the line of communication between London and Aylesbury, and in near approach to the King's quarters during the war, had seen as much soldiering as any town in the county excepting St. Albans.' The greatest scare came in June 1644, when the Royalist army marched across Buckinghamshire into Bedfordshire.

Instead of continuing eastward, however, the King's forces moved towards Aylesbury. Thus the threat to Hertfordshire and London came from the north-west, not the north.

Parliament had a resourceful commander in General Browne; he mustered 4,000 men at Dunstable—3,000 from Hertfordshire and Essex, and 1,000 from London. Kingston continues the story:

. . . with the blare of trumpet and beat of drum, they marched up what is now West Street to the Downs, along the old historic Icknield Way . . . to Tring and Berkhamsted with no cavalry escort. There was an uninterrupted view of the enemy's country over a line of hills extending from Leighton Buzzard by Mentmore to Aylesbury, and there was nothing for it but to risk the march and meet Colonel Norton's 500 horse from Windsor at the Berkhamsted rendezvous. Along the road from Watford are travelling for the same rendezvous the stores of powder, bullet and match and £10,000 in money to pay the troops with, ordered by Parliament.

Not a battle, not even a skirmish, occurred in this district, but the townspeople often had to provide free quartering and provisioning, and large numbers of soldiers were billeted even in small cottages.

In 1648, St. Peter's Church was turned into a prison and hospital for prisoners from the siege of Colchester. General Fairfax gave orders that they were not to be starved. To mitigate the horror of huddling together so many maimed, hungry soldiers, the windows were taken out; a few months later the vestry levied a special rate of twopence an acre to pay for the replacement of the glass.

One of Cromwell's bravest soldiers was Daniel Axtell, who was born here in 1622. His father, William Axtell, was a chief burgess; in 1639 he was town clerk. Apprenticed to a London grocer, Daniel came under the spell of preachers and politicians, gave up his trade, and shouldered a pike for Cromwell. Captain, major, then lieutenant-general of a foot regiment at the age of 26, he was prominent in many a spell of hard fighting. In the summer of 1648, when soldiers of his own county were chasing the Cavaliers through Hertfordshire to the battle of St. Neots, he distinguished himself in the siege and capture of Deal Castle. At the trial of Charles I he was captain of the guard.

This young soldier from Berkhamsted must have been detested by a young woman who, like Axtell, was born in 1622. Anne, daughter of Thomas Murray, spent some of her early years at Berkhamsted Place. She figured in a successful plot to send the young Duke of York (afterwards James II) to Holland when the Royalist cause was all but lost. The boy was whisked away from St. James's Palace during a game of hide-and-seek, rowed down the Thames to a riverside house, and dressed as a girl. Anne Murray obtained the garments, which included a scarlet petticoat, from a tailor; he was astonished by the unfeminine measurements. Anne was among the people who bade farewell to the duke, who looked 'very pretty' as he embarked for Holland and many years of exile.

The execution of Charles I sent a shiver of revulsion throughout the land. Anne Murray described it as 'that execrable murder never to be mentioned without horror and detestation,' and was so afraid that some terrible catastrophe would overwhelm London that she hurried away to the country.

Many staunch Parliamentarians were equally shocked by the King's execution. A Berkhamsted man, Nathan Paine, declared at a wedding feast that he regretted ever having fought with the Parliamentarians. The execution of the King was 'the most horrid murder that ever any history made mention of'; it was a plot worse than the gunpowder treason, and there was no difference but that one was under and the other above ground. Had he known what would happen he would never have drawn his sword for Parliament, and would never do so again.

For speaking 'in a spiritt of malice,' Nathan Paine and two other men, Thomas Aldrich and Nathan Partridge, were brought before the bailiff and chief burgesses by an order from the Council of State. They were acquitted, and continued to play an active part in the life of the town. Paine was a churchwarden in 1658, and Aldrich was bailiff in 1655.

They lived to hear the church bells ring and fireworks explode in

1660, 'the happie yeare of King Charles the Seconds restauration to his Government,' to quote an entry in the churchwardens' accounts. The parish spent 10s. on 'a barrell of beare' and 15s. 2d. on powder and match. The bellringers received £1.

Anne Murray, too, rejoiced at Charles II's 'restoration', though having been deprived of her interest in the lease of the manor of Berkhamsted she was forced to sell all her jewellery. In 1685 she received a pension of £100 a year from James II, a belated recognition of the part she had played in his escape from London in 1648. Anne died in 1699, leaving behind diaries which tell of her romances, her exploits and above all her efforts to serve the Stuarts. She wrote several religious works and a friend wrote her biography.

Daniel Axtell, the dashing young Cromwellian soldier, saw service in Ireland after the Civil War; as Governor of Kilkenny he was among the many ill-chosen administrators who poisoned Anglo-Irish relations for generations to come. In 1656 he resigned his commission and returned to England to 'live upon the estates which he had acquired in the Service.' For a time he returned to his native town, not to the modest house in which he was born but to the mansion on the hill, Berkhamsted Place, previously the home of the Murrays.

In 1660, Axtell was arrested and tried as a regicide. Witnesses agreed that at the trial of Charles I he had shown undue prejudice, ordering the guard to point guns at a woman who cried, 'Oliver Cromwell is a traitor!' After a dramatic trial he was sentenced to death, and the scene at Tyburn was no less dramatic than the trial. Axtell stood in a cart, the rope round his neck, ready for the cart to be drawn away and leave him swinging from the gallows, but the carman declared that he would lose his horse and cart rather than have a hand in the hanging of such a man. Bible in hand, Axtell told the hushed crowd that the cause he had followed was the cause of the Lord; 'I ventured my life freely for it, and now die for it.' Eventually the common hangman had to perform the task the carman had refused.

Daniel Axtell continues to arouse great interest in the United States. His brother Thomas emigrated to New England, and his descendants formed a family association. A book entitled *The Axtell Heritage* shows how greatly both Daniel and Thomas are still revered. Many American members of the Axtell family have visited Berkhamsted.

The restoration of the monarchy was followed by renewed persecution of dissenters (p. 38) and a brief, rare period of disarmament. The church chest contains a document which refers to 'An Act for raising of seven score thousand pounds for the compleat disbanding of the whole Army and paying off some of the Navy.' Hertfordshire was required to raise £2,800, and Berkhamsted's share was £22 19s. 4d. But it was not long before the militia was reorganised, and demands poured in for larger contributions, particularly for 'the speedy building of ships of war' to fight the Dutch.

Besides making direct contributions toward the cost of the Army and Navy, the town was required to supply soldiers and arms. In 1669 the 'musquetiers' of Berkhamsted were ordered to appear at St. Albans, 'compleatly armed,' taking with them three days' pay, 6d. for the mustering, half a pound of powder and half a pound of bullet. Eighteen townsmen were responsible for equipping the six soldiers; among the 'ffinders of the armes' was Thomas Payne, son of the outspoken Nathan. The pikes, swords, muskets and other arms were kept in St. Peter's Church.

A strange episode at the time of the Monmouth Rebellion (1685) provides a sporting postscript. Thomas Wells informed the magistrates that William Norman and Joseph Mills, with two others, 'came over to him and ask him to play football, but that was not the business; 'twas to goe and be listed for the Duke of Monmouth.' The footballers were bound over.

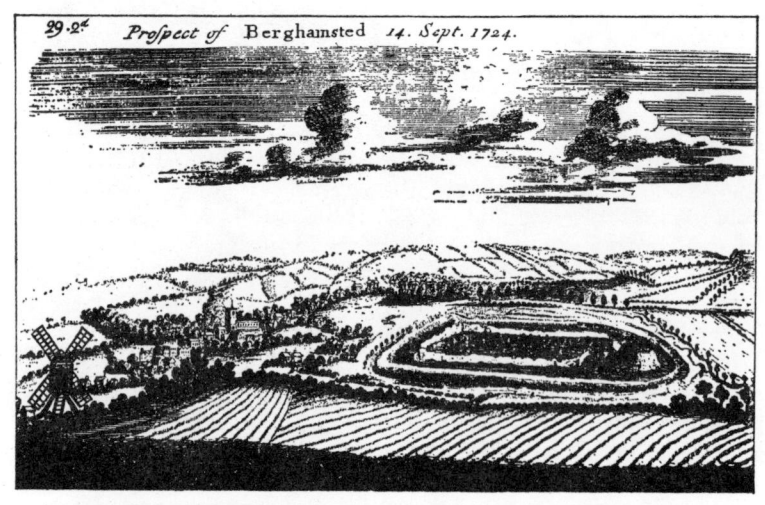

The Windmill (Millfield), Church, Castle and Berkhamsted Place

Egerton House (p. 110), where railway workers who introduced Methodism to Berkhamsted held their first meeting. The Rex Cinema occupies the site of this Elizabethan mansion

Above: The 'Gamma' airship (p. 27) in the Castle grounds, 1913

Below: The cattle market in the early 1900s

Above: High Street, showing Court Theatre, c. 1920

Below: The Inns of Court Regiment marching back to camp after church parade 1916

The Sayer almshouses, 1830, long before Cowper Road was made

XIII
The Sayer Almshouses

THE NAME of a seventeenth century benefactor is familiar to all who pass by the almshouses at the corner of Cowper Road. An inscription boldly proclaims 'The Guift of John Sayer, Esq., 1684.'

He was a kinsman of the Rev. Joseph Sayer, rector of Northchurch from 1675-93, and died at Berkhamsted in 1682. His tomb in St. Peter's Church states that he was head cook to Charles II, to whom he constantly attached himself in difficult times, at home and abroad. In other words, he was in exile with the King during the Commonwealth.

Among Sayer's acquaintances was Samuel Pepys, the diarist, who recorded the following on September 9, 1661:

> I went with Captain Morrice into the King's Privy Kitchen to Mr. Sayers [sic], the Master Cook, and there had a good slice of beef or two to our breakfast; and from thence he took us into the wine-cellar where, by my troth, we were very merry, and I drank so much wine that I was not fit for business.

As the king's head cook, John Sayer received £150 a year and £40 for livery. Charles, however, was dilatory in paying his servants, and Sayer sometimes had to ask for the payment of arrears. There were other occasions when Sayer lent money to the king. Obviously with private means, Sayer was able to take the lease of Berkhamsted Place and thereby became steward of the manor. His interpretation of certain ancient rights upset many parishioners; the rector, churchwardens and others complained to the king that Sayer had unjustly detained market and other tolls which previously had helped to maintain the church, school and poor of the parish.

The Court of Exchequer decided in favour of Sayer, whose motive, according to a report to the Treasury, was solely to preserve the king's right. Such benefits as arose, chiefly out of the tolls and profits of the market, were small, and Sayer always gave them back to the town, 'the better to preserve peace and amity among his neighbours.'

Sayer bequeathed £1,000 for building almhouses and for the relief of the poor of the parish. The will, dated July 2, 1681, directed that the money was to be used 'as the said John Sayer shall appoint in writing,' or, in the event of his death before making any such appointment, in accordance with the desires of his wife, Mary Sayer. John died in 1682, before he had prepared a scheme, and Mary, who survived him by nearly 30 years, not only drew up elaborate instructions but also augmented the bequest by several hundred pounds.

An almshouse 'consisting of twelve rooms, designed for the habitation of six poor widows . . . allotting two rooms to each widow,' cost £269. The large balance was invested in land and the annual income devoted to the needs of the almswomen and other poor parishioners.

Candidates for rooms were not considered unless they had lived for ten years at least in Berkhamsted or Northchurch, and were 'of good fame, constant frequenters of divine service as by law established in the Church of England, and aged 55 years at the least.' The trustees were empowered to evict the poor widows for any misdemeanour.

It must have been rather touching to see the old ladies, all dressed alike, walking to church every Sunday morning and afternoon, 'going orderly two by two according to their several ages, the oldest going last.' In church they were required to 'behave themselves devoutly during the whole time of divine service and sermon.'

They were forbidden to take in lodgers, or to 'lodge out of the said almshouse in any other house whatsoever in the said town of Berkhampstead St. Peter or in the parish of Berkhampstead St. Mary.' But if an almswoman wished to go away from the town to visit friends, she could apply for permission to do so from the trustees, who never granted that permission to more than one almswoman at a time or for a longer period than one month in a year.

Upon the youngest of the six widows fell the duty of assisting other almswomen in case of sickness. She was also required to 'keep the court clean between the wall and the house,' and to unbolt and bolt the outer gate each morning and night at a fixed time.

Every three years the widows were entitled to new cloth gowns, 'of 20s. value at least.' In 1828 the price was £1 8s. 9d. per gown, 'and the women do not now receive them quite so often.'

Several changes in the administration of the charity have been made. Although retaining the original frontage, the almshouses now accommodate four widows, each with three rooms, instead of six widows who each had two rooms.

Another almshouse, restored in 1966, adjoins the churchyard of St. Mary's, Northchurch. Usually known as the Church House, it was granted in 1590–1 to Sir Edward Stanley, having been in the tenure of a man named Axhill—probably Henry Axtell, who, Chauncy states, was a rich man who starved himself and was buried at Northchurch in 1625. In 1654, according to a deed of trust from John Edlyn, the house was 'to continue and be for an habitation to the Aged and Poor.' Thirty years later it was 'full of poor people, viz. five several families.'

XIV
Literary Links

THE REGISTER of baptisms in St. Peter's Church contains the following entry: '1731, Dec. ye 13, Willm ye son of John Cowper D.D., rector of this Parish, and Anne his wife, was baptised.'

The extremely large script that was used for this entry almost suggests that the clerk had the gift of foresight, for William Cowper became a famous poet, hymn and letter writer. One of his biographers, Robert Southey, thought that Berkhamsted would be 'more known in after ages as the birthplace of Cowper than for its connection with so many historical personages who figured in the tragedies of old.'

In fact, interest in the poet and his works has declined sharply in modern times. Even in the town of his birth his name is seldom mentioned. It was not like that in Victorian times and the early years of this century. William Cowper was the subject of many a public lecture, and schoolchildren were left in no doubt that Berkhamsted had produced a very great poet whose works deserved a place on every bookshelf. Members of learned societies came here on literary pilgrimages, and if they expected to see his birthplace they were disappointed. The house Cowper preferred to a palace was

The old Rectory, birthplace of William Cowper

pulled down by John Crofts, rector from 1810–50, and a new rectory was built higher up the hill; this is no longer the home of the rector, for whom a smaller house was built on the site of Cowper's birthplace.

John Cobb, rector from 1871–83 and local historian, did his best to arouse interest in the poet; he raised funds for the Cowper memorial window in St. Peter's Church and provided an inscribed marble slab on the much-photographed 'Cowper's Well' in the rectory garden; this well no longer exists.

So many good biographies of William Cowper are available that it would be pointless to do more than refer to the poet's connection with Berkhamsted. His father, instituted rector in 1722, and his mother, a descendant of the poet John Donne, had more than their share of sorrow; five of their seven children were lost in infancy. The final tragedy came in 1737 when Anne Cowper died shortly after the birth of the seventh child, John.

William was then six years old. He had attended a small private school in the town and was transferred to Dr. Pitman's boarding school at Markyate. Shy, sensitive and physically weak, he was the victim of horseplay and bullying and was so scared of a senior boy that he came to know him better by his shoe buckles than by his face. At the age of ten he was sent to Westminster School, where Warren Hastings was one of his schoolfellows.

William Cowper spent many holidays at Berkhamsted. As we know from his letters and poems, he knew and loved the family home and the surrounding countryside. He was eighteen years old when his father died in 1756, and stayed here for several months. Many years later, in a letter to a friend, he wrote:

> A sensible mind cannot do violence even to a local attachment without much pain. When my father died I was young, too young to have reflected much. He was rector of Berkhamstead, and there I was born. It has never occurred to me that a parson has no fee-simple in the house and glebe he occupies. There was neither tree, nor gate, nor stile in all that country, to which I did not feel a relation, and the house itself I preferred to a palace. I was sent for from London to attend him in his last illness, and he died just before I arrived. Then, and not till then, I felt for the first time that I and my native place were disunited for ever. I sighed a long adieu to fields and woods, from which I once thought I should never be parted, and was at no time so sensible of their beauties, as just when I left them all behind, to return no more.

In another letter, dated 1788, Cowper said:

> ... at Great Berkhampstead, the place of my birth, there is hardly a family left of all those with whom, in my earlier days, I was so familiar. The houses, no doubt, remain, but the inhabitants are only to be found now by their gravestones; and it is certain that I might pass through a town in which I was once a sort of principal figure, unknowing and unknown.

On receiving a portrait of his mother, he wrote:

> I heard the bell tolled on thy burial day,
> I saw the hearse that bore thee slowly away,
> And, turning from my nurs'ry window, drew
> A long, long sigh, and wept a last adieu!
>
> . . .
>
> Where once we dwelt, our name is heard no more,
> Children not thine have trod my nurs'ry floor;
> And where the gard'ner Robin, day by day,
> Drew me to school along the public way,
> Delighted with my bauble coach, and wrapp'd
> In scarlet mantle warm and velvet cap,
> 'Tis now become a history little known
> That once we call'd the past'ral house our own.

'Gard'ner Robin' was Robert Pope, the rector's gardener, and the school was on the site now occupied by part of Sharland's store, 212 High Street.

A writer of several well-known hymns, Henry Twells, was a curate of Berkhamsted in the mid-nineteenth century. Once a week he walked to Frithsden to conduct services in a cottage, and on one occasion, due to illness and accident, he was the only person present. It is said that Twells walked back to his lodging in Castle Street and there, thinking of the sick, wrote the first draft of 'At even, ere the sun was set.'

A woman novelist, Maria Edgeworth (1767–1849), spent part of her girlhood in a Georgian house between Gossoms End and Northchurch. Edgeworth House was probably built in 1767, though there are Elizabethan bricks in the foundations. In 1776 it became the home of Richard Lovel Edgeworth, a writer with an inventive mind who filled the rooms with ingenious gadgets. He also filled his home with children, of whom there were nineteen.

Maria, the eldest child, must have been well qualified to write a book entitled *The Parent's Assistant*. Her tales for young people were widely read, but today her reputation stands upon such novels as *Castle Rackrent* and *The Absentee*.

Visits to Northchurch during school holidays were remembered by Maria when, with her father, she wrote *Practical Education* and described a visit to Peter the Wild Boy.

Turning to modern times, one of the most widely read novelists in the world, Graham Greene, was born here in 1904; his autobiography, *A Sort of Life,* contains many references to his years at Berkhamsted School, of which his father was headmaster from 1911–27.

One of Graham Greene's contemporaries at school was Peter Quennell, the poet, critic and biographer; his parents, C. H. B. and Marjorie Quennell, lived in the town and collaborated in a series of educational books, including the very popular *History of Everyday Things in England.*

The distinguished historian, Dr. G. M. Trevelyan, lived in Berkhamsted and was active in the acquisition of Ashridge properties for the National Trust. Another noted historian, Dr. Esmé Wingfield-Stratford, wrote many books in his home in Cross Oak Road. W. W. Jacobs, the humorist and short story writer, lived in Chesham Road.

In 1904-7, J. M. Barrie, the dramatist, was a frequent visitor to the Llewellyn Davies family at Egerton House, where members of the original cast of 'Peter Pan' entertained his hosts' children, one of whom, Peter, inspired the play. Long after the original Peter had grown up, Barrie was asked to use his influence to save Egerton House from demolition, but he was then too ill to intervene and the Rex Cinema replaced a handsome though much neglected Elizabethan house.

John Cobb and Henry Nash

Two writers who achieved no more than local fame will be remembered and quoted as long as interest is taken in the town's history.

Shortly after arriving here in 1853, the Rev. John Cobb, an energetic and popular young curate, made an intensive study of local history and gave two long lectures to the Mechanics' Institute in 1854. A year later he published his *History and Antiquities of Berkhamsted.* By that time Cobb had moved to Northchurch, staying there as curate until he was appointed Vicar of Kidmore End, near Reading, in 1863. On returning to Berkhamsted as rector in 1871, he resumed his interest in local history and added much interesting material as appendices to his second edition, which appeared shortly before he died in 1883.

In the preface to the second edition Cobb mentions 'most especially my old friend Henry Nash,' author of *Reminiscences of Berkhamsted* (published in 1890). Nash drew upon an excellent memory and intimate knowledge to provide a fascinating account of life and events in Victorian Berkhamsted. He was a founder of the Mechanics' Institute, a member of the School Board, and probably did more than anyone else to establish Berkhamsted School for Girls. It was typical of the man who helped so many others to make their mark in life that he was well content with the modest income provided by a little shop in Castle Street which supplied leather to the many practical bootmakers of the period. Little more than 5 feet tall and a cripple from birth, Henry Nash in late Victorian times was known as the Grand Old Man of Berkhamsted. He died in 1899.

XV
Some Unusual People

THE STRANGEST character in local history was of German origin. He lived in the parish of Northchurch for nearly sixty years, and throughout that time was known by the name which appears on his gravestone near the porch of St. Mary's Church, 'Peter the Wild Boy.' As extraordinary as the man himself was the interest that was taken in him by royalty, novelists, pamphleteers, journalists, moralists, and scientists. Daniel Defoe wrote an account of his early life, and it is thought that Peter gave Dean Swift some ideas for his Yahoos in *Gulliver's Travels*. Long after the wild boy's death, Dickens mentioned him in *Edwin Drood* and *Martin Chuzzlewit*.

In July 1725, a farmer found a boy, about twelve years of age, in a field near the Pied Piper's town of Hamelin. He was naked but for tattered remnants of a shirt around his neck, and ran away on seeing the farmer. Two apples held at arm's length eventually enticed him into the town of Zell, where he was placed in a hospital.

No one knew how long the boy had been living in the fields and woods, feeding on roots, fruit, buds and acorns. The power of coherent speech, if he had ever possessed it, had been lost.

At Zell, Peter was said to have rested, animal fashion, on his knees and elbows. He disliked wearing clothes and preferred to walk barefooted. Stories of his antics reached the city of Hanover when George I was there in November 1725. The King ordered the boy to be brought to him; he was ushered into the royal presence at dinner-time, and rejected delicacies from the King's table until offered raw meat, which he devoured with relish.

The *St. James's Evening Post* of December 14, 1725, reported that Peter walked on his hands and knees, climbed up trees like a squirrel, and fed upon grass and moss. This was the first of many highly coloured reports to appear in English newspapers, but really sensational reporting did not start until George I returned to England, bringing Peter with him at the request, according to one account, of the Princess of Wales, shortly to become Queen Caroline.

Until the novelty wore off, the Court was delighted with its unusual pet. Peter was sent to Harrow—not to the famous school but to a boarding house for boys kept by a Mrs. King. Fellow boarders had to share the company of an uncouth lad who wandered around eating onions as though they were apples.

As the memorial tablet in St. Mary's Church states, the ablest masters were provided for Peter, 'but proving incapable of speaking or of receiving instruction, a comfortable provision was made for him by Her Majesty at a farmhouse in this Parish, where he continued to the end of his inoffensive life.'

Peter's arrival in this district was due to Mrs. Tichborne, one of the Queen's bedchamber women, who arranged for him to stay with Mr. and Mrs. James Fenn, of Haxter's End Farm, Broadway, Mr. Fenn receiving an allowance of £35 a year from the Crown for the boy's maintenance.

Peter may have been inoffensive, but his low standard of intelligence, and especially his lack of a sense of direction, caused Mr. Fenn much anxiety. In 1745, it is said, Peter wandered afar and was arrested on suspicion of being a spy for the Pretender; his inability to explain that he was the celebrated wild boy apparently convinced his captors that he was a wild Highlander! According to the *Gentleman's Magazine* of 1751, Peter roamed as far as Norfolk and was imprisoned at Norwich as a sturdy vagrant. Fire broke out in the Bridewell and Peter enjoyed the spectacle so much that he was reluctant to be rescued from the blazing building.

Thereafter he wore a heavy leather collar with a brass rim bearing the inscription: 'Peter, the Wild Man from Hanover. Whoever will bring him to Mr. Fenn at Berkhamsted, Hertfordshire, shall be paid for their trouble.' This collar is preserved at Berkhamsted School with part of a petition to the King from Mr. Fenn for a larger allowance in view of the expense of advertising for Peter and returning him when he wandered far from home.

For thirty years Peter stayed at Haxter's End; then, on the death of the farmer, he moved to Broadway Farm and his new guardian was Thomas, James Fenn's brother. When Thomas Fenn died, Peter stayed on at Broadway with Farmer Brill.

That Peter was once taken to London, by royal command, shows that he was not completely forgotten by the Royal Family. For this visit he was shaved and dressed in the livery of the King's servants. His effigy was on view at a waxworks in the Strand in 1774.

Peers and commoners called to see Peter at the farm. He was able to utter a few words and the farmer and his wife put him through a ritual to show his powers of speech and understanding to visitors. He could sing 'Nancy Dawson,' and on hearing music he clapped his hands, threw his head about in a wild, frantic manner, and sometimes danced until he was exhausted. Visitors often gave him money, which he immediately passed on to his keepers; this perhaps explains why they were always ready to receive callers.

Some accounts say that Peter was never mischievous, others that he would sometimes tear his bedclothes to pieces and run threateningly after people who teased him. He was sullen at the approach of

Peter the Wild Boy

Victorian carpenter

John Ghost, Victorian gravedigger

Victorian charwoman

Above: The water-mill which gave Mill Street its name (p. 82)

Below: Billet Lane, the old road to Dunstable, in 1888; there was only a plank bridge over the Bulbourne

bad weather, loved a roaring fire, even in midsummer, and acquired a liking for beer and spirits. Occasionally he visited a gin-shop at Berkhamsted, 'where the people treated him.' He hated physic unless it was liberally flavoured with gin, and could not bear the sight of the apothecary who attended him.

Peter sometimes helped the farmer, and it is said that while assisting his master to fill a dung-cart he was left alone to finish the work. Soon the cart was filled, but Peter was determined to keep on working, and started emptying the cart. He failed to understand why the farmer was displeased on finding all the work undone.

Gossipers and jokers no doubt made up tales to amuse themselves and to give visitors a few more things to talk and write about. The then headmaster of Berkhamsted School, the Rev. Thomas Bland, was so incensed by 'men of some eminence in the literary world [who] have in their works published strange opinions and ill-founded conjectures' about Peter that he contributed his own 'true account' to Northchurch parish register.

Peter died at the age of about seventy-two and was buried at Northchurch. The brass tablet in the church was paid for by the Treasury.

Polly Page

In the historical pageant of 1966, an innkeeper's daughter was seen paying a tearful farewell to Louis XVIII as he left Berkhamsted in a magnificent coach-and-four on the second stage of his journey to France. For this romantic scene there was no need to resort to fiction; the exiled French king was a great admirer of Polly Page of the King's Arms Inn.

Mary (nicknamed Polly) was born in 1787. Her father, John Page, moved into the King's Arms at the right time to benefit from the Coaching Days. Of the three daughters who helped him to run the inn, none was so fair as Polly. Henry Nash extolled her 'unvarying attention, charming manners and great conversational powers.' Such was her knowledge of the aristocracy that she 'held the peerage at her tongue's end and could trace the pedigree of almost every family of note that honoured her with a call.'

Polly was about 20 years old when she met Louis XVIII for the first time. After wandering from one country to another, he came to England and established his court at Hartwell House, near Aylesbury. On frequent journeys to and from London he always contrived to see Polly Page while the horses of his coach were changed, and habitués of the Kings Arms were not to be denied a little gossip.

For seven years Louis lived at Hartwell. Then, in 1814, the fall of Napoleon opened the way for his return to France. The end of 24 years of exile was marked by celebrations at Aylesbury, where six young men mounted their horses to form a small bodyguard on the first stage of the king's journey to London, Dover and Calais. There were cheers, cheers, all the way.

The leader of the king's bodyguard was a young man named Fowler, who had attended Berkhamsted School and was said to have been the only Aylesbury resident who spoke French fluently, a facility which made him the confidant of many members of the exiled court. His son, J. K. Fowler, wrote *Echoes of Old Country Life* in 1893 and said it was 'well known that a quarter of an hour or so would be spent in the ostensible act of changing horses while the king would flirt with the fair Polly.'

After bidding Polly farewell and inviting her to visit him in France, Louis continued on the next stage of his journey to Stanmore, where, at the Abercorn Arms, the Prince Regent, several royal princes from the Continent, officers of state and a guard of cavalry assembled to meet him.

And Polly did indeed go to France. She was the king's guest at the Tuileries and returned home with 'many valuable souvenirs of the interesting event, which were treasured with as much care as family relics.'

But again the gossipers were unkind to Polly, and she published a denial of the scandalous rumours that were circulating about her friendship with Louis. A newspaper cutting dated October 1830, preserved at the County Record Office, Hertford, states that Polly's conduct was 'perfectly correct.' She had been 'as remarkable for meeting with extraordinary circumstances as for maintaining an irreproachable character in the course of her life.'

The writer of the article added that Polly was married to a young man of property whose guardians applied to the Ecclesiastical Court for a dissolution of the marriage, and obtained a sentence of nullity on account of the young man being under age and not having had the concurrence of guardians at the time of the marriage. The report continues:

> Miss Page brought an action against her quondam husband, Mr. Monk, for breach of marriage-promise, and the quondam wife obtained a verdict against the man who had formerly been her husband, with considerable damages. To complete the character of these singular proceedings, which romantic as they appear are not coloured, it may be added that the latter proceedings were, it is said, promoted and assisted by a character no less curious than the occurrences themselves—the late eccentric Earl of Bridgewater.

Diaries kept by William Buckingham, steward to the seventh Earl of Bridgewater (who, unlike his uncle and his brother, was *not* eccentric) show that the Earl often visited the King's Arms and was a friend of Polly Page.

She remained 'mine hostess' of the King's Arms after the death of her father in 1840. In the following year she received Queen Victoria and the Prince Consort when they called while the horses were changed. This event so excited her sister Sarah that she collapsed and died. Mary died in 1865, over seventy years after her father had moved into the King's Arms.

John Tawell

In early Victorian times a prominent and indeed conspicuous townsman was John Tawell. He always wore the Quaker's traditional long cloak and broad-brimmed hat, and during his five years in Berkhamsted took an active part in parochial affairs.

The townspeople did not know that Tawell, a Norfolk man, had been convicted of forgery in 1813 and transported to Sydney, where his good service in a convict hospital earned him a free pardon. He then started his own business as an apothecary, and was joined by his wife and two children. Though expelled by the Society of Friends, he built a meeting house in Sydney in 1835.

In 1839 Mrs. Tawell died under somewhat mysterious circumstances; poisoning was suspected by those who knew of his affection for Sarah Hart, who had been engaged as a nurse for his wife.

Returning to England, Tawell installed Sarah Hart, by whom he had two children, in a cottage near Slough. Then, in 1841, he married, at Berkhamsted registry office, a widow named Sarah Cutforth, who had kept a private school for girls in the town. Living in good style at the Red House, the couple was so greatly esteemed that neighbours believed it was a case of mistaken identity when Tawell was arrested. But in Aylesbury Crown Court the life story was told of a humbug who, to save money and preserve his 'respectability', had poisoned his mistress, Sarah Hart. Despite a clever attempt to cover up his tracks after committing the crime at Slough, he was arrested in a London coffee house, sentenced to death, and hanged in Aylesbury market place in 1845, having gained extra notoriety as the first murderer to be caught as the result of a message transmitted by a new marvel of the age, the electric telegraph.

Snooks the Highwayman

Strictly speaking, a highwayman named Snooks belongs to the history of Boxmoor, but his Berkhamsted connections are sufficient to justify his inclusion among the town's unusual characters. Legend has it that he worked for a time as an ostler at the King's Arms Inn, and if that was so his employer, John Page, was destined to meet him in an official capacity on the day of his death, for the King's Arms landlord was also high constable of the Dacorum Hundred.

Snooks was not without local knowledge. He had information that on a certain night the postboy who took the mailbags from Tring and Berkhamsted to Hemel Hempstead would carry banknotes of great value.

John Stevens, the postboy, was jogging along the highway on his mare when Snooks flourished a pistol and ordered him to 'Stand and deliver.' Stevens meekly obeyed, and Snooks seized the mailbags. One letter alone contained £500.

Labourers found the rifled mailbags and reported the crime to John Page, who immediately galloped to London. At the General Post Office, he delivered the rifled mailbags to Mr. (afterwards Sir) Francis Freeling, and for a time the authorities were without a clue as to the identity of the robber.

Meanwhile, Snooks found lodgings in Southwark and spent some of the smaller banknotes. Then he made a literally fatal mistake. He sent a servant girl to purchase some cloth, warning her to bring back the right change from a £5 note. But it was a £50 note! Having aroused suspicions, Snooks hurried away, and the police soon discovered that the £50 note had been taken from the Tring and Berkhamsted mailbags.

A substantial reward, said to be £300, was offered for information that would lead to the highwayman's arrest. Snooks was captured at Hungerford, sent to Hertford for trial, and sentenced to death. John Page was instructed to find a place for the highwayman's execution near the scene of his crime between Bourne End and Boxmoor, and thousands of people made a morbid holiday of the occasion on March 11, 1802. He was buried in a field, and many years later the Boxmoor Trustees provided the gravestones that are still visible from the railway and road. The inscription gives his name as Robert Snooks, but he was indicted in the Christian name of John, and in the Berkhamsted constables' book the following entry appears: 'Attending the execution of James Snook, £0 10*s*. 0*d*.' The Berkhamsted constables at that time were William Shakespeare and John Bailey; three years earlier a Berkhamsted constable was John Stevens, who may or may not have been the postboy who was told to 'stand and deliver'.

XVI
Customs and Legends

IN YEARS GONE BY many a strange story was told of witches and highwaymen, of secret tunnels and ghosts, of odd characters and strange cures.

Long-remembered tales, passed on from one generation to another, ceased to find eager audiences long before the cinema, radio and television provided a new, unlocalised diet of drama and humour. Old customs, too, were discontinued. May Day, so important a date in Merrie Berkhamsted that the churchwardens paid a man one shilling 'for cutting and carrying in the maypole' in 1622, was celebrated half-heartedly in late Victorian times and then not at all. And not since the early years of this century have the bounds of the parish been beaten.

An interesting custom was maintained until men no longer cut and carted away gorse and fern from Berkhamsted Common. At nightfall, on the last day of August, they made their way to the Common, and at midnight—it was said that they listened for the chimes of the parish church clock a mile away—the men staked claims in the manner of gold prospectors.

The cutters of gorse and fern were obeying an ancient order 'that no person whatsoever shall cut or cause to be cut any fern on the common called Berkhamsted Common from the first day of June until the first day of September yearly.' This was to prevent damage to the life and recuperative powers of the fern; restrictions were also imposed on the size of the cutting implements.

No logical reason can be found for 'Cock-hat Sunday,' formerly celebrated by the boys of Berkhamsted School on the last Sunday but one of term. Every boy was supposed to go to church with his hat on one side. On Oak Apple Day, any boy who failed to put a sprig of oak in his buttonhole was liable to be slapped with a bunch of nettles.

In Victorian times, on Christmas Day, St. Peter's Band climbed the 100 steps to the top of the church tower to play carols and salute the happy morn. To welcome the new year, revellers joined hands with worshippers who had just left the watchnight service and sang 'Auld Lang Syne' under the churchyard yew. This midnight custom survived until the 1939–45 war.

In the seventeenth century, when few people had watches and clocks, the sexton was paid £1 a year to ring the church bell at 4 a.m. and again at 8 p.m. There were protests when this custom was allowed to lapse.

People living near the church did not care for a very rare bird, a whistling weathercock. Perched high above the tower, it was fitted with reeds and whistled shrilly in high winds. After an irate parishioner had fired his gun at the weathercock and scored a direct hit, the reeds were plugged to silence the bird, which is now perched on a window sill near the vestry, not much the worse for his injuries.

Cobb, our Victorian rector and historian, mentions a curious tradition to the effect that St. Paul came to Berkhamsted and 'drove away from it for ever all serpents and thunderstorms.' The sight of a snake in the district is certainly rare.

Like Berkhamsted, Northchurch formerly held a 'statty' (statute) fair in the High Street. The village also celebrated 'Betty Jenks' birthday' on the Thursday after Whit Sunday, when John Thorne, who lived in Duncombe Road (then called Thorne's Yard), summoned children to run races up and down the yard for packets of sweets. It is possible that this little tradition was started by, or was in memory of, the wife of the Rev. David Jenks, rector of Northchurch from 1778-93.

For many years a spring known as St. John's Well was thought to have certain properties which healed sore eyes. Many a bottle of the precious water was taken away for home treatment. The spring was a popular source of drinking water in medieval times, and wardens were appointed to regulate its use. In 1400 they prosecuted washerwomen for polluting the water. But this was a petty offence compared with the worshipping of nymphs and sprites at the well; Hugh of Grenoble, Bishop of Lincoln (1186-1200) came to Berkhamsted to stop those pagan ways.

St. John's Well took its name from a leper hospital which formerly occupied the Post Office site; the water ran down St. John's Well Lane to join the Bulbourne but ceased to flow in the 1930s. Thus we no longer have an opportunity of testing its curative properties and the town has lost whatever chance it had of becoming a spa.

A more important but spasmodic tributary of the Bulbourne, the Bourne Gutter, is our local woewater, said to flow only in times of war or rumours of war. It is now assumed that abnormally rainy seasons cause the Bourne to flow. For most of its journey this intermittent stream determines a mile or two of the county boundary; it joins the Bulbourne at Bourne End, giving the village its name.

In addition to a curative well, Berkhamsted possessed a curative tree. Sufferers from the ague were advised to bore a hole in the trunk of an ancient oak tree at the top of Cross Oak Road, peg a lock of hair in the hole, and then spring away, leaving the hair behind. This shock treatment was actually tried, as holes, pegs and hair testified, but apparently there was no cure for the resultant baldness.

To cure fits, victims were advised to ask a clergyman for a silver coin which had been presented as a sacramental offering, have the coin made into a ring, and wear it on a certain finger.

Not for many years has a Berkhamstedian been bewitched, but in the great days of witchcraft no less a person than the last bailiff of the borough was famous for his success in removing evil spirits. Dr. Christopher Woodhouse prescribed 'stinking suffumigations' and unpalatable concoctions. One of his patients, Mary Hall, daughter of a Little Gaddesden blacksmith, 'would tremble and shake, and so continue all the while the Antidaemonic Medicines boiled.' Dr. Woodhouse's course of treatment included the placing of Mary's nail-parings in the chimney.

The devil no longer rattles his chains on Berkhamsted Common, near Potten End water-tower, as was once believed. Perhaps he was the very same devil who was credited with the making of Grims Dyke, the ancient earthwork on the Common. Some golfers may still subscribe to this interesting theory.

A pleasanter story from Berkhamsted Common concerns Carl Linnaeus, the eighteenth century Swedish naturalist, who walked beside the golden gorse and knelt down to thank God for the beauty of the scene. This act of thanksgiving is said to have taken place in several other parts of the country, but if there is no evidence that Linnaeus came to Berkhamsted, it is known that one of his disciples, Pehr Kalm, stayed for some time at Little Gaddesden.

On the far side of the Common is the pleasant village of Potten End. According to an unkind and unauthenticated story, the villagers left their doors open whenever flocks were driven through the village, in the hope that a sheep would step inside and provide free meat for several days to come.

Potten Enders were nicknamed Cherry Pickers, but the great cherry centre was nearby Frithsden, where the place-name Cherry Bounce has outlived most of the trees. A cherry fair was held there annually, but by late Victorian times it consisted of nothing more than a brief sale of fruit in a barn and a visit to the Alford Arms. Frithsden has a hazy, disputed claim to have originated the cherry turnover. The children of the hamlet, employed to scare birds off cherry trees, used loud rattles and sang this indelicate air:

> Shoo birds away
> Fer tuppence a day
> Through 'edges 'n' ditches
> You little black bitches.

An elderly Frithsden man named Rose dreamed that a chest of gold lay buried at the bottom of a pit and that it would be his if he could reach it without speaking a word to break the spell. He took into his confidence a young neighbour, and after hours of digging, their spades struck a metallic object. So excited was the younger man that he uttered a naughty word; the sides of the pit caved in and the men were almost buried alive. And so the chest of gold remains to this day, awaiting disciplined diggers who remember that silence is golden.

The steep, narrow road between Frithsden and Nettleden, known as Spooky Lane, is where Henry I is said to have been thrown from his horse and trampled on by a mare ridden by a monk. This story, passed down through the ages, bears some resemblance to the account of Randulph, Henry I's chancellor, being trampled on by a horse when on the way to Berkhamsted Castle with the King (p. 20).

Between Northchurch and Dudswell stand two old cottages named Dropshort. This curious but not rare name is said to have arisen from a mistake on the part of the builders; they were told to erect the cottages farther along the road, but 'dropped short' of their destination. Another version is that bricks fell off the back of a cart and were put to good use on the spot. The smaller cottage was in fact a very expensive form of bus shelter, kept clean and warm by the tenant of the larger cottage so that Thomas Smart, a former owner of Norcott Court, could wait in comfort for the stage coach or his own carriage. Many rich people who lived some distance from the highway had similar lodges, and 'dropping short' of one's destination explains the name Dropshort.

Many years have passed since anyone has seen the ghosts of Cromwell's army along the valley still known as Soldiers' Bottom. This must have been an awesome sight: spectral Ironsides marching at dusk, their pikes glittering in the rays of the dying sun. Were they on the way to Wigginton, where Cromwell's men, according to legend, trained their cannon on Berkhamsted and destroyed the castle? A good story is spoiled by the fact that the castle was ruined before Cromwell was born.

Houses and an inn on the south side of the High Street are said to have subterranean links with the crypt of the parish church. Another secret tunnel, from the castle to a former hilltop mansion, Berkhamsted Place, has been attributed to the Black Prince, though it is difficult to understand why he or anyone else required a tunnel between two buildings which did not exist contemporaneously. Excavations for sewers, water, gas and electricity have failed to expose a medieval underground system.

XVII
Local Names

MANY people have argued about the derivation, spelling and pronunciation of the town's name. *The Place-Names of Hertfordshire,* a most informative book, states that Berkhamsted is the 'birch-grown homestead,' but other works of reference support the view of John Norden (1598) that Berkhamsted was so called because it is situated among the hills. Both derivations make sense. A third suggestion, that the name means 'the fortified homestead,' is no longer favoured.

John Cobb, in 1855, amused himself and his readers by finding fifty different spellings in old documents, from the time-saving Bercam to the extravagant Berkehampstedde. But there have been hundreds of versions ever since Anglo-Saxons produced the spelling Beorhðanstædæ. A twentieth century printer or typist can be just as inventive as a scribe of olden times.

Berkhamsted was not born Great but had greatness thrust upon it by clerks who feared that the town would be confused with Little Berkhamsted, a village near Hertford. Thus the town was called Great, Greate, Much or Muche Berkhamsted; perhaps the nicest version was Berkhamsted Magna. By Victorian times most of the inhabitants had dropped the word Great, but the Great Berkhampstead Urban District Council did not prune its title until 1937.

Spellings such as Barkehamsted (1546) and Barkhamsted (1644) show how the name was pronounced in Tudor, Stuart and indeed later times. Hertford, of course, has been pronounced Hartford for centuries, and 'Hurtford' is now considered rather coarse, but Chauncy thought otherwise in 1700:

Doubtless it was merely called Hartford for Hertford, by reason of the broad dialect and ill-speaking of the vulgar sort of people, which oftentimes through long usage changed the true names of divers places.

Some of the vulgar, ill-speaking people crossed the Atlantic and spelt names as they were pronounced; in Connecticut there is a township of Barkhamsted some 25 miles from the state capital, Hartford. In Old England we do not 'bark' the town's name; anyone who calls it Barkhamsted is assumed to have come from another planet. The first syllable is stressed, and many people do not sound the aspirate, i.e., *Berk*'amsted, not Berk*ham*sted.

Berkhamsted is in a district noted for Ends—Potten End, Gossoms End, Bourne End, Heath End, Water End and dozens more within a radius of ten miles. John Godsalm (1287) and his descendants, who used many spellings, gave Gossoms End its name;

an amusing version is Goshams yende (1565). John Potyn (1565) may have named Potten End. Reginald Asselyn (1314) is linked with Ashlyns, Hugh Harefot (1200) with Haresfoot, Adam Durant (1294) with Durrants, and Robert de Cruce (1307) with Cross Oak, though old Berkhamstedians maintain that Cross Oak Road (formerly Gilhams Lane) takes its name from a rather famous oak which once stood at the Shootersway crossroads.

Shootersway was Sugarsway in the eighteenth century; by earlier names it does not sound so sweet. Shokersweye (1357) and Shukerswaye (early 1600s) is believed to have been a robbers' way, a lonely and presumably dangerous alternative to the highway in the valley. Shootersway formerly continued from Brickhill Green (originally Brick Kiln Green) through Sandpit Green (Sandputtes, 1300) and Long Green to Bourne End, where the name Sugar Lane survives. The Bourne Gutter joins the river Bulbourne at Bourne End, hence the name of the village.

From early times a large, densely wooded part of Berkhamsted Common was called The Frith. Frithsden means the valley belonging to the wood or frith; in 1406 and in later documents it was spelt Freseden, and some older folk still pronounce the name accordingly.

Dodeswell (1269) is now Dudswell, a spring probably named after a man named Dodd. Rotheway (1432), Northcote (1300) and Kyngeshill (1427) are now Rossway, Norcott and Kingshill. The road to Kingshill, appropriately named King's Road, was formerly known as Bridewell Lane, after the gaol which once occupied the police station site. In still earlier times King's Road was Cocks Lane. 'John Cockes tenement with a backside at Cocke's Lane end' is mentioned in a survey of 1607.

Chesham Road has changed its name on at least two occasions. It was Elwynslane in 1525 and Grubslane in 1608. Castelstrete (1357) is more easily recognised than Ravenyngeslane (also 1357); Raven's Lane takes its name from a family which provided the Black Prince with one of his henchmen.

Three Close Lane was the way to three closes or paddocks where sheep and cattle on the way to London markets were penned for the night. Highfield Road (Hifield in Henry VIII's reign) was popularly known as the Pightle, an old name for a strip of land between two copses, and in Victorian times part of the road was called Prospect Place. Manor Street is so called because the land was formerly part of the Pilkington manor estate; the manor house stood opposite Rectory Lane.

Kitsbury is a contraction of Kitts End Bury, sometimes spelt Kicks End Bury. Doctors Commons Road is a name which arouses curi-

A SHORT HISTORY OF BERKHAMSTED

osity; it is a reminder of Doctors Common, which extended from Cross Oak Road to the road which now bears the common name. Greneweyfyld is mentioned in 1357; it extended from Shrublands Road to the road named Greenway. The town's most interesting name, St. John's Well Lane, recalls a long-vanished leper hospital dedicated to St. John and a spring which formerly sent water trickling down the lane. Mill Street and Bank Mill Lane (Northmullane in 1357, Banekmull in 1269) take their names from ancient watermills. A long-forgotten windmill named Millfield (le Mulfield, 1357), on the east side of Gravel Path, which was so called because carters came that way with loads of gravel from the Common.

The local authority annoyed local historians by changing the ancient, honourable and appropriate name of Back Lane to Church Lane. To be fair to the council, names of local historical interest are sometimes used for street names; in 1971 a new road was called St. Edmund's to perpetuate the name of a field off Chesham Road. The names of local worthies are also used for street names—Cowper, Torrington, Bourne, Edlyn, Brownlow, Bridgewater, Egerton, etc. Cowper's most popular poem inspired the name of a road called Gilpin's Ride. Another happy choice was Captain's Walk. Captain Constable-Curtis already had Curtis Way named after him; he lived in a former mansion called The Hall, the name of which is preserved in such roads as Hall Park and Hall Park Hill.

Hony Lane, Sparrow Lane, Benethenstrete, Ragged Row and Tiptoes Lane are among the names found in old documents. Tiptoe was an old family name. Formerly there was a Petticoat Lane in the Park; Happy Valley was the name of a cluster of tiny cottages off Castle Street; Snob's Alley was the forerunner of Prince Edward Street; the shortest right of way of all, between High Street and Back Lane, deserves the nameplate 'Post Alley' to perpetuate the name that was used when the post office was next door. The row of shops in front of Back Lane (Middle Row) was nicknamed Grab-all Row, not because the tradesmen were rapacious but because their premises were built on the old market place—a case of land-grabbing several centuries ago.

Old field names include Strawberry Close, Dilly Piece, Goodspeeds, Gilliflowers, Timber Close, Kentish Croft, Partridge Close, Oxfield, Spark Field, Shepherd's Close, and Broken Post Meadow. Poor crops and poverty are suggested by Hunger Hill, Little Starve Acre, Ragged Jack and Stony Bottom. Dog Kennel Field now bears a much larger structure, Berkhamsted School for Girls, and Maiden's Baulk is part of the boys' playing field.

XVIII
Manorial and Parochial Boundaries

THE MAP of the manor of Berkhamsted, printed on the end-papers of this book, is reproduced from *Berkhamsted Frith, or Common, and Ashridge in the Nineteenth Century,* a book written by Lady Marion Alford (p. 98) and printed 'for private circulation only' in 1878.*

The map shows the boundary of the manor as defined in a survey conducted by Sir John Dodderidge in 1607. Especially interesting are the place-names mentioned in the survey, starting at Lyons Corner, near the north-west corner of the manor, and continuing to North Wood, Ashridge Park Corner, Prince Hatch, Stoney Lane, South Wood, Swilley Pond, Grymes Ditch, Sherman's Bound, Sale Pits Pond, The Pykes, Pitmead Corner, Hockeridge Bottom, Mill Field Wood, Bachelors Grounds, Round Green, Sutton Mead, Hawcroft Deane, Hitchin Gate, Nunne Corner, and so to Lyons Corner.

The parish boundaries, indicated by a dotted line, show that St. Peter's extended beyond the manor into a portion of Ashridge Park and also to Frithsden and Potten End. The parish boundary ran through Ashridge House. Another curiosity is an isolated portion of Northchurch parish near Frithsden, also beyond the boundary of the manor.

A line from A-B and C-D indicates the central portion of the Common enclosed in 1866.

The map deserves very close study, preferably in comparison with a modern map. Of especial interest is the very small built-up area; even after the railway had been opened, there were few houses beyond High Street, Castle Street, Water Lane, Mill Street and the lower part of Highfield Road.

---

*Lady Marion Alford wrote this book to explain the Brownlow case for the enclosure of part of Berkhamsted Common in 1866. She said:

My object in writing a true version of facts which have been placed before the world in a garbled form, either intentionally, or through ignorance, is to show exactly the position in which my eldest son [the second Earl Brownlow] was placed, his actions and motives.

He can no longer defend himself, or judge whether silence or truth will, in the long run, be most likely to revive controversies, which at one time caused much ill-will.

Those who knew him best have deemed it unnecessary to vindicate his character as a country gentleman, a neighbour, and a landlord. During his short life he made many friends, who can bear witness to his unselfish, generous nature, his earnest desire to ameliorate the condition, and to add to the pleasures of his own people, and of the poorer classes in general.

FOR FURTHER READING

JOHN COBB'S *History and Antiquities of Berkhamsted* (first edition 1855, second edition 1883) and Henry Nash's *Reminiscences of Berkhamsted* (1890) have been sufficiently praised in this book to create an even stronger demand for the few copies which still exist in the County Library. Both books have been out of print for many years, as have G. H. Whybrow's *History of Berkhamsted Common* (1934) and R. A. Norris's *Berkhamsted St. Peter* (1923).

Of all the county histories with chapters on Berkhamsted, by far the best is the *Victoria History of Hertfordshire*, vol. II, which first appeared in 1908 and was reprinted in 1971. Local historians are also indebted to such early writers as Sir Henry Chauncy, the Rev. N. Salmon and R. Clutterbuck. John Cussans' *History of Hertfordshire* (1879) is of especial interest to genealogists.

Augustus Smith of Scilly, by Elizabeth Inglis-Jones (Faber and Faber, 1969) is a splendid biography of Berkhamsted's defender of common rights.

The lavishly produced *History of the College of Ashridge*, by Archdeacon Todd (1823) is extremely rare; many fine plates make it a 'collector's piece.' *The Bridgewater Millions*, by Bernard Falk (Hutchinson, 1942) should be read by everybody interested in Ashridge; it contains much information, presented in a very lively style, about the Bridgewaters and Brownlows.

Vicars Bell's *Little Gaddesden* (Faber and Faber, 1949) is a very good village history, with many references to Ashridge. Mr. Bell also wrote *To Meet Mr. Ellis* (Faber and Faber, 1957), giving an entertaining account of the activities of the eighteenth century farmer-author who lived at Little Gaddesden.

Hilltop Villages of the Chilterns, by David and Joan Hay (Phillimore, 1971) is an extremely readable and lavishly illustrated account of four villages just over the Buckinghamshire border, Cholesbury, Hawridge, St. Leonards and Buckland Common.

Booklets of local interest include *A Short Account of Thomas Bourne*, by R. A. Norris (1929), *The Memorial to John and James Murray in Berkhamsted Church* by R. A. Norris (1937), *The Berkhamsted Institute*, by P. C. Birtchnell (1945), and *The Town Hall and Market House*, by P. C. Birtchnell (1960).

Index

Adult education, 55
Agriculture, 68
Akeman Street, 82
Alford, Lady Marion, 98
All Saints' Church, 35
Almshouses, 105-6
Ashlyns, 50
Ashridge, 90-93, 101
Axtell, Daniel, 102, 103

Baldwin, Thomas, 40
Baptist Church, 38
Barrie, J. M., 110
Becket, Thomas, 20
Belgic remains, 11
Berkhamsted, Henry of, 23, 32
Berkhamsted Place, 27, 101
Black Prince, 22, 90
Bonhommes, 90
Borough of Berkhamsted, 56
Boundaries, parochial, 29
Bourne Gutter, 118
Bourne, Thomas, 51
Breweries, 73
Brickhill Green, 98
Bridewell, 58, 63
Bridgewater, Countess, 92
Bridgewater, third Duke, 84, 91
Bridgewater, seventh Earl, 92
Brotherhood of St. John, 39, 45
Brownlow, Earls, 93, 95
Brushmaking, 70
Bulbourne, river, 82
Butts Meadow, 99

Canal, 84
Cary, Sir Edward, 24, 27
Castle, 18-27
Castle Street, 13, 18
Charles I, 28, 61, 100
Charles II, 59
Charters, royal, 56
Chaucer, Geoffrey, 23
Chesham, 88
Churches, 29-38
Church House, Northchurch, 106
Churchill, Baroness (Mrs. Winston) 49
Churchwardens' accounts, 41
Cicely, Duchess of York, 23
Cinemas, 16
Civil War, 101
Coaching Days, 84
Coat of arms, Berkhamsted, 56
Cobb, Rev. J. W., 110
Coldharbour enclosure, 94
Common, Berkhamsted, 94-98
Congregational Church, 38
Constables' accounts, 43

Cooper, William, 72
Coram, Thomas, 50
Cornwall, Duchy of, 22, 94, 95
Cornwall, Earls and Dukes of, 21 22, 90
Corporation of Berkhamsted, 13, 57
Court House, 59
Cowper, Ann, 32
Cowper, William, 107
Crafts, 68-74
Cross Oak, 118, 122
Cures, curious, 118

Documents in church chest, 40
Domesday Book, 12
Dropshort, 120
Duchess of York, Cicely, 23
Duchy of Cornwall, 22, 94, 95
Dupré, John and Thomas, 47

East, Job, 70
Eastmead, Thomas and Elizabeth, 52
Edgeworth, Maria, 109
Edlyn, John, 36
Edlyn, William, 94
Edmund, Earl of Cornwall, 22, 90
Edward, Black Prince, 22, 90
Edward III, 22
Egerton House, 110
Elizabeth I, 33, 91
Enclosure of Berkhamsted Common, 94
Evangelical Church, 38
Evening Schools, 55

Fairs, 77
Farming, 68
Finch, General, 28, 53
Fitz Piers, Geoffrey, 21, 39
Foundling Hospital, 50
Friends' Meeting House, 38
Frithsden, 119, 120, 122
Fry, Dr. T. C., 48

Gaveston, Piers, 22
Geoffrey, Fitz Piers, 21, 39
Greene, Graham, 109
Grims, Dyke, 11

'Harvey Coombe' (locomotive), 87
Henry of Berkhamsted, 23, 32
Henry VIII, 90
High Street, 82
Highwayman (Snooks), 115
Hospitals, 39

Incent, John, 45
Industries, 68-74
Inns, 79

Inns of Court Regiment, 16
Isabella, Queen, 21, 39

Jacobs, W. W., 110
James I, 56, 57, 61

Kitchener's Field, 99
Kitsbury, 15, 35, 122

Lace manufacture, 70
Lane's Prince Albert apple, 72
Legends, 117-120
Linnaeus, Carl, 119
Louis, Prince, 21
Louis XVIII of France, 113

Malt manufacture, 68
Manorial courts, 59
Marlin Chapel, 37
Market, 75
Methodist Church, 38
Millfield, 123
Mills, water, 82
Monmouth rebellion, 104
Moor, The, 99
Mortain, Robert, Count of, 12, 18
Motor-cars and motor-cycles, 89
Murray, Anne, 102, 103

Names, local, 121-123
Nash, Henry, 110
National Trust, 98
Newspapers, local, 74
Norman Conquest, 12
Northchurch, 11, 35, 44, 59, 62, 66, 106, 118, 120
Nugent, Rev. George, 62

Page, John, 81, 116
Page, Mary ('Polly'), 113
Paine, Nathan, 102
Park, Berkhamsted, 99
Paxton, William, 95, 97
Pepys, Samuel, 105
Peter the Wild Boy, 36, 111
Place-names, 121-3
'Polly' Page, 113
Poor Law, 61-63
Population changes, 15, 16, 17
Press, local, 74
Prison, 58, 63
Public-houses, 79

Quennell, C. H. B. Marjorie and Peter, 109

Railway, 85
Randulph, Chancellor, 20
Raven, John, 32, 122
Registers, parish, 43, 44
Richard of Cornwall, 21

Robert, Count of Mortain, 12, 18
Roman Catholic Church, 37
Roman remains, 11

St. Mary's Church, 35
St. Michael and All Angels' Church, 37
St. Peter's Church, 29
Sacred Heart, Church of the, 37
St. John, Brotherhood of, 39, 45
Sanitary Authority, Rural, 64
Sayer, John, 28, 105
St. John's Well, 118
Schools, 45-55
Sheep dip, Cooper's, 72
Shootersway, 122
Shops, 77
Siege of Castle, 21
Ship Money, 100
Snooks the Highwayman, 115
Sparrows Herne Trust, 83
Spelling of Berkhamsted, 121
Stevens, Thomas, 89
Street names, 121-3
Smith, Augustus, 48, 54, 96
Straw-plaiting, 71
Sunday schools, 54
Sunnyside, 66

Tawell, John, 115
Three Close Lane, 122
Timber trade, 69
Torrington, Richard and Margaret 33
Town Hall, 77
Tramway, proposed, 88
Trevelyan, Dr. G. M., 110
Turnpike, 83
Twells, Henry, 109

Urban District Council, 16, 65

Vestry, 60
Victoria School, 55

Waltham, John of, 34
Watercress, 73
Waterhouse, Thomas, 90
Wethered, Francis, 50
Wild Boy, Peter the, 111
William I, 12
Witchcraft, 119
Wingfield-Stratford, Dr. Esmé, 110
Woodenware, 69
Woodhouse, Christopher, 59, 119
Wool merchants, 69
Workhouse, 61
World War I, 16
World War II, 17

Yeoman, John, 14, 84

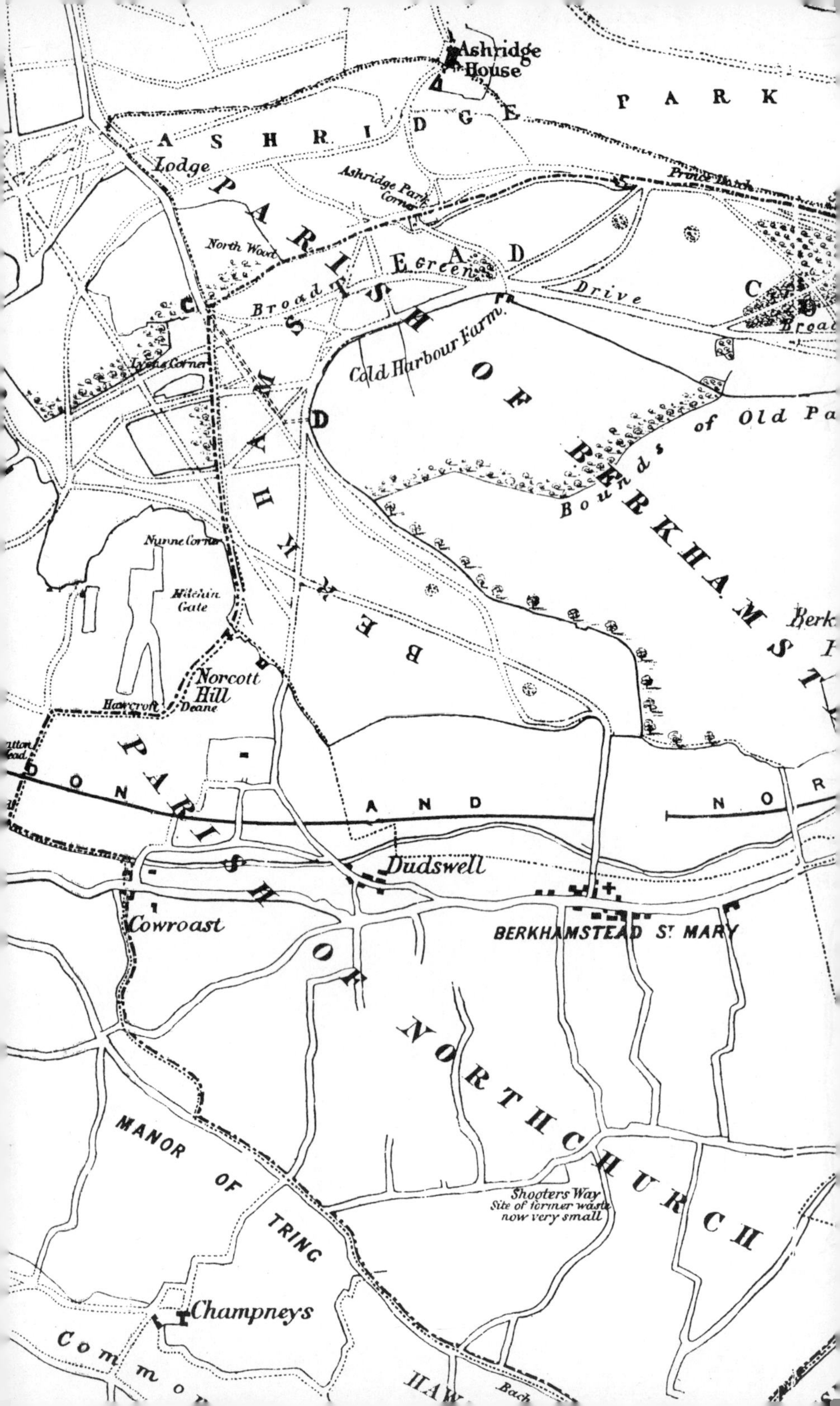

Ashridge House
ASHRIDGE PARK
Lodge
Ashridge Park Corner
North Wood
Broad Green
Drive
Cold Harbour Farm
Bounds of Old Pa
Norcott Hill
Deane
AND
Dudswell
Cowroast
BERKHAMSTEAD ST. MARY
PARISH OF NORTHCHURCH
MANOR OF TRING
Shooters Way
Site of former waste
now very small
Champneys